The Key To
YOUR
Unknown
TALENT

*The new kind of progress which makes
human traits and abilities the subject rather
than just the source of change will dominate
the agenda of the next century,
perhaps even the next decade.*

G. OWEN PAEPKE, *THE EVOLUTION OF PROGRESS*

The Key To
YOUR
Unknown
TALENT

A new discovery about <u>you</u>!

DONALD E. SEYMOUR

✦

TALENT DISCOVERY PRESS
MILWAUKEE, WISCONSIN

Copyright © 1996 by Donald E. Seymour

Publisher's Cataloging-in-Publication Data
Seymour, Donald E.
The key to your unknown talent: a new discovery about you / Donald E. Seymour.
p.   cm.
ISBN 0-9647532-0-0
1. Ability.   2. Vocational guidance.   3. Vocation.
I. Title.
BF431.S49   1996
153.0—dc20   95-90449

PROJECT COORDINATION BY JENKINS GROUP INC.

Printed in the United States of America
10 9 8 7 6 5 4 3 2 1

To my wife, Donna Lou Seymour

Tell me whom you love,
and I'll tell you who you are.
—Old Creole proverb

Contents

PART III - IN SUPPORT OF TALENT DISCOVERY

Foreword

by John Buuck, Ph.D.

One of the many gifts bestowed to humans is that each individual has one or more talents. Most of these individuals could be successful in more than one field if they were able to match their talents with the proper occupation. However one of the tragedies of life is that too many people do not discover the talents they possess. As a result, there are individuals moving from one job to another because they are not challenged, interested or qualified in the work they are doing.

As the author states, there are an estimated over 40,000 occupations in existence today. Add to the fact that perhaps ten percent of the occupations that will be available in the year 2000 have not even been developed at this date. Twenty years ago very few people were involved in occupations that used a computer. Today most occupations require at least some knowledge of this technology. The same will be true twenty years from now. Many people will be involved in the newly-developed occupations. Therefore it is imperative that individuals discover their talents today hidden somewhere in those 40,000 occupations.

As president of Concordia University Wisconsin, I see so many students entering the university today not being able to declare a major in their early university career simply because they are unsure of the occupation they want to pursue. While vocational interest tests given by the vocational counselor can be of benefit to some, more and better help is needed for the student. This book will provide valuable information towards helping not only students but individuals in all walks of life.

The author, after a number of years of thoughtful insights and personal experience, has provided the reader a clear understanding of what talent is and provided the reader tools for talent discovery. Whenever a new creative idea is presented there will always be those who have doubts. However, *The Key to Your Unknown Talent* can unlock the hidden talents of many individuals if they will carefully follow the process presented in the book. The talent discovery process itself could one day further open wide the doors to discover individual talents.

On the surface, Donald E. Seymour may be an unlikely individual to develop the ideas for the discovery of one's talent given his educational background as he shares it in the book. However once he discovered some of his own talents he became a very successful businessman in an area that would normally require a college degree in several scientific fields. This attests to his intelligence and creativity and gives credibility to his work.

I have had the privilege of knowing Mr. Seymour for many years. Over the past several years he has shared the unfolding of his thought process toward discovering one's talent. This book is the culmination of his thinking. I am confident that there are many people who by reading this book will discover some of their own talents which will lead to a successful occupation or avocation, and as a result, a more enjoyable life.

John Buuck, Ph.D.,
President
Concordia University Wisconsin

Acknowledgments

The author is indebted to many people for their advice and encouragement. Thanks go to Connie Amos, Sue Armstrong, Paul Bailey, Dr. John Buuck, Michelle Gagne, Art Jurack, John Komivas, Al Malkasian, Warren Meyer, Jory Prosen, Mike Puzia, Bob Senninger, Donna Seymour, Greg Seymour, Gwen Shannon and Mike Sullivan.

Special thanks to Chris Roerden who did the first stage editing. The people at The Jenkins Group Inc., Mark Dressler who started the book on its way, Alex Moore who guided the book into fruition and Mary Jo Zazueta who did the final critique and editing and took a personal interest. The time and help is much appreciated by the author and hopefully will be appreciated by all people who can benefit from Talent Discovery.

Author's Note

Prepare yourself to read this book. This is unknown territory we are entering, many accepted and ageless principles may fall. As an example. The individual has been conditioned to accept their station in life and that others are much more capable, talented and intelligent than they. The individual has not been educated to believe that they may have specific and discoverable hidden talents.

What if those principles, among others we were taught to accept, are wrong? What if we have been going down the wrong road for the last few generations as the age of technology passed us up? What if these principles have blinded us and therefore we humans have not been able to cope with all the major problems we now face.

As you read this book you will find the talent discovery concept is foreign to the form of thinking that we have been taught for generations, it will therefore require new and different thinking and reasoning.

No one can question that if talent were discoverable, people should then be educated according to their capabilities. There is a problem: we do not have the tools to help people find their talents, so we cannot educate an individual according to his/her talents. To know how to develop the tools, a new and perhaps radical career selection method to find talent has to be found.

Following this search for your talent may require you to push aside the cob webs of educational conditioning you have grown up with. You may have to open your mind and for the first time to allow yourself to see you as you really are, what you have to work with, what important things you can do and what responsibilities may be the result.

Talent discovery is going to be highly controversial, shockingly revealing and completely foreign to the way of thinking we have been taught to accept as its message cuts across many professional and scientific lines, making new reasoning difficult to defend.

As an example, the research I have done leads me to suspect that all people are endowed with equal intelligence and ability . . . ?

In this search I have chosen to present the events just as and where they happened, that you may understand how I arrived at the conclusions I did. It is important for the reader to be exposed to how I felt, thought, deduced and reacted, just as they may have under the same circumstances. The search for talent discovery because of the lack of previous research, led me down a diverse path into a vast unknown territory. It was when I was far away from home and business that I could relax, let my mind wander and allow it to dwell on this unusual thirty five year interest I had in talent.

It is now August 25, 1993. I am standing on a wooden porch outside the rustic Denali Park Hotel in the Alaskan wilderness. The air is glacial cool as I gaze in the distance at majestic Mt. McKinley, over 20,000 feet high. It is inconceivable that something so massive could be pushed up that high in the stratosphere. As I gaze at the mountain my mind turns to what is for me a massive and overwhelming undertaking . . . writing the book on Talent Discovery, I know that I must complete when I go back home. I seem to have no choice, the question is always before me.

Who has unknown talent and is it discoverable?

Before you answer that question and perhaps come to understand and even believe, it is necessary for you to follow the string of events resulting in what appears to be a most consequential talent deduction. A talent discovery method if found will touch on you and those you care about and the lives of all humans, now and far into the future, probably more than individuals have ever been affected before. It is therefore important for you to accumulate all the knowledge you can about talent.

Do you have unknown talent? I believe you do and I believe it can be found.

Introduction

Your talent is what you are, the crown jewel of your genetic structure. There may be special talents that you have always possessed that you do not know you possess that may be equal to the best. Every individual may have special capabilities in specific areas, in which they can perform certain tasks better than any other activities. If others are capable of a high talent capability then why not you? Perhaps you were not short changed, special talents may be a natural trait we all have.

Your greatest asset may be a talent that could maximize your work ability and income, a talent that could enhance your leisure time enjoyment and improve the quality and purpose of your life.

People have a desperate need to find their own identity and self worth. Talent is the one asset that each person possesses that once discovered can provide positive identity and self worth.

Our government has far too many serious problems: sociological, economic and environmental, and our planet too is awash in problems for which there seems to be no answer. All these problems are so degenerating that we are mesmerized by the hopelessness of finding solutions. The problems are not abating but continue to escalate. (In more and more communities throughout the country people are fearful of their personal safety and have stopped leaving their homes at night.) Talents can solve problems. One newly discovered talent could solve one vital problem, ten would have a better chance and ten thousand new talents applied to a vital problem could surface a wave of talent that few problems could withstand.

New discovered talents could provide the jobs and income needed to free untold numbers of people from poverty's net, resulting in many of society's problems fading on their own. People who currently receive financial assistance from the government could become taxpayers. This reversal could reduce our government and deficit; lowering taxes for all. In addition to vital problem solving, discovered talents in all our people could produce a wave of new inventions, products and services, thereby expanding employment opportunities.

Although you may be in an occupation you love, are comfortable with and even talented at, you may have other talents that would amaze you! Discovering your hidden talents may be healthier for you and bring you greater joy and interest for the rest of your life: it may also enhance your present occupation.

Each individual has a treasury of talent that he or she desperately needs to find to solve personal problems. To survive business needs to find the treasury of talent it has in all of its employees. Our government needs to find the treasury of talent in all of its people to solve its problems.

The sources of most problems are people and only people have the ability to solve problems. Rather than concentrating on developing new tools to limit problems at the source (the hidden talents of the people) our government is concentrating on treating the problems. The value of the problem solving ability and benefits of our undiscovered talents makes one wonder why we aren't pulling all stops to find a way to discover individual talent?

We have no choice but to find the best talent in each of us and to match those talents with the many occupations that will open the talent doors to the innovators and problem solvers we so desperately need. Our personal problems, societies' problems and the ominous threat to Earth's life support system make it imperative that an all-out effort be made to find a way to discover the unknown talent in all our people. It is the last asset we have left to solve the problems. Our future freedom may depend upon it.

The U.S. Department of Labor has catalogued and coded 20,000 basic occupations. This list could be revised and expanded to include a total of over 40,000 different job classifications. It is not possible for a person to work at and experience each of these occupations to find the right combination of activities in which his/her talent capability lies. Even if such exposure were somehow possible it is most unlikely that an individual would be able to qualify their best talents as to health, success or continuing interest. There has to be another way of discovery and qualification of talent.

Are you highly talented in some unknown activity or occupation that you born with and may never discover? If you had such a talent that could make a contribution to society, wouldn't you want to know what it was?

There can be no doubt that talent discovery is a new science, the next frontier . . . the most interesting and challenging frontier of all. It will dominate conversation far into the future. The question will be asked . . . can we find and develop a talent discovery method in time?

Join me in this search for your most valuable asset . . . your unknown talent?

PART I

✦ ✦ ✦

SETTING THE STAGE

Man possesses much more than he knows.
MARIA MONTESSORI

1

Talent, Skill, Genius and You

*I have for several years now been engaged in a
search for truths about myself and my life;
many other people are doing the same. More
people than ever are asking, "Who are we?
What is our purpose?"*
SENATOR AL GORE, *EARTH IN BALANCE*

Very likely you have genius capability or an unknown talent
that, once discovered, could improve the quality of your life
dramatically. Since the words talent, genius and skill are often interchanged, it is necessary to distinguish between them before
proceeding further.

In ancient times people who appeared to have genius were said
to have a "gift of the gods." In more recent centuries, people believed that Galileo, Newton and Leonardo da Vinci possessed a special spirit, and were honored and blessed with special powers by the
gods. Yet, other people who appeared to be gifted (and who challenged accepted principles and dogma) were crucified for having
powers of the devil.

To this day most people are in awe of and are puzzled by this
phenomenon. Audiences make heroes out of a strange assortment
of seemingly gifted people. We identify great inventors, artists and

musicians as geniuses. All of them work in highly visible occupations.

Is genius limited to people in glamorous occupations? Is it limited to people who are in the spotlight? Is reputation a requirement of genius? If so, then genius takes on a different meaning. Genius then describes an individual who has been fortunate enough to discover a natural talent and has the opportunity to exploit that talent in a highly visible field. Are there geniuses in bricklaying or dictation? I believe there are, but who knows or cares enough to recognize them?

Genius has been found in the most unlikely people, in the most unusual places and under the most unusual circumstances. A native in a remote area of New Guinea who has never seen a violin can hardly become a violin genius, even though he or she may have the talent. A dropout in the inner city of St. Louis might have become a world renowned scientist. A person selling drugs in the ghettos of New York might have the talent to discover a cure for cancer. But, without the opportunity to realize their talent, how could they or we ever know?

Exposure and environment are important. When individuals come in contact with an activity that is close to their natural talent and they have the opportunity to use the talent, they typically show surprising ability.

Genius can be a wonderful accident or a difficult burden. In some instances it may not take superhuman effort to become a genius; however, work, sacrifice and dedication are often required to develop and maintain it.

Geniuses are not genius at everything. They are limited to their own talents. Geniuses have their personal problems like you and me. Is it possible that geniuses are normal, hard working people, who perhaps have only been fortunate in finding their own talent? (I take nothing away from those referred to as "genius," they set new standards in our civilization and culture.)

Webster defines genius as: "a man intellectually endowed. That disposition or bent of mind which is particular to every man and which qualifies him for a particular employment." Notice Webster says "every man." Is that possible?

When we examine geniuses, we may find that they excel by utilizing their natural traits. In the few instances in which genius surfaces, it may simply be an accidental exposure of a hidden talent.

It is not logical that special geniuses are born. God creates people and He creates them genetically alike. The fact that some people are fortunate enough to find themselves close to their natural talent pattern (either by intuition or accident) may not make them a genius, but rather it may make them fortunate.

Skill and Talent

Skill is the ability to do something well. It is more often associated with physical rather than mental dexterity; however, some skills do require much thought. Skill is a practical and repetitious activity, one that can be learned over time. Skills need not be compatible with an individual's talent.

Talent is more than skill. It is a special ability, a mental endowment or capacity of a superior kind. Talent appears to be inborn and genetically particular to each individual.

My purpose is not to study genius or skill. The goal is to help people find their best calling—the calling that is their talent. This is where we will begin the search for natural talent—a most valuable possession—that when found may provide the identity so desperately wanted and needed by so many people.

2

Selecting Talent

*Once we've cleared away mistaken impressions of
who we ought to be, we're better prepared to
discover who we are.*
PETER KLINE, THE EVERYDAY GENIUS

To determine what talent is, it may be helpful to first examine
how society selects and identifies the most talented individuals:

+ Musicians and vocalists are judged and selected by their peers.
+ We select top talent in the arts by judging.
+ Coaches select talented players for team sports by observa-
  tion, and trial and error.
+ Individual athletes are identified by winning their respective
  contests. The selection is automatic.
+ We identify talent in business by results.
+ The public identifies talent with money (by purchasing works
  of art, certain automobiles, etc.) and by attending events
  (concerts, movies, theatrical events, etc.).

Selection by Observation

A high school decides to have a football team. The school board hires a coach, and encourages students to try out for the football team. Every student who attends the first practice session thinks or hopes that somehow he/she is good enough to make the team.

The coach selects his team by observing the players in action. His objective is to select the best athlete for each position. The coach's only chance for a successful team is to observe each of the students practice in all of the positions: quarterback, defensive end, outside receiver, guard, center, etc. Through observation the coach can decide who performs best in each position.

This trial and error method takes weeks of practice sessions. Although each student had a pre-conceived notion of his/her abilities it is the coach as an observer, and not the student, who is the best judge.

Was the individual student qualified to know where his/her abilities could best be used by the team? Probably not; yet, every year we expect the same type of judgment from college students when they select the major that they will pursue. Students try desperately to select a course of study that seems best for them. They probably have no indication of what talents they have, and often their course selection is an expensive gamble. These college students do not have the benefit of a trial and error occupation selection process by a coach.

Some college instructors try to help their students make proper course selections, but the ability that the student has in the instructor's classroom may only show a study interest, not a talent. Even the career assessment tools that exist only indicate interests, not talents.

When looking for employment the same is true. Most people choose an occupation that they have experience in, is available to them or pays best. Millions of people select where they will work and what profession they will pursue for the remainder of their lives without the benefit of knowing talents they may have. What chance does a person have of selecting an occupation that best suits them without this information?

With so many occupations to choose from, is it possible for students and workers to make their course and job selections by observation and trial and error? In reality, no. Considering that there are only twenty-two different positions on a football team, we cannot logistically put every individual through the same type of occupational selection process to find an occupation that best suits the individual's talents. Trial and error observation of one individual adequately trying out 40,000 different occupations would take thousands of years.

Additionally, the process of selecting football players does not necessarily mean that these are the most talented quarterbacks, centers, etc. Rather it only indicates that of the students who tried out for the team, certain individuals appeared best able to fill the available positions.

What can we conclude by examining our current methods of selecting talent? The chance of achieving any semblance of efficient occupation selection with our existing career assessment tools is almost impossible. Existing career selection methods cannot match an individual's talent with the great many occupations because no method of identifying individual talent exists.

None of these selection methods identifies an individual's best talent. In this era of high technology our methods of identifying and selecting talented individuals remains primitive.

Career guidance methods do not show us what talents an individual has. Is there some way we can expose an individual to all existing occupations to find their best talents?

3

Author's Exposure

To a large extent individual behavior is influenced
by the amount and quality of training received and
degree of health, strength, intellect and talent a
person is born with.
JAMES ALBUS, BRAINS, BEHAVIOR, AND ROBOTICS

Before we proceed it is important you know something about
my education, my business career, and how and why I be
came interested in the search for talent discovery.

I did not take well to formal education. I found most of it boring, and it took me an extra semester to graduate from both grade
school and high school (occasionally I failed my english and arith-
metic classes). In the ninth grade I started to spend all of my spare
time composing stories, novels, poems, and essays; which was strange
as I disliked my english classes. My grammar and punctuation were
so poor, I was ashamed to let anyone read what I had written.

Between the ages of twelve and thirty-two I held over one hundred part-time jobs; often three at a time. This was not so unusual,
as many people did the same during the Depression of the 1930s. I
can recall standing in a long line of men and boys at five-thirty in
the morning, all of us hoping to get a job for even a few hours
weeding a carrot farm for ten cents an hour.

Between the ages of eighteen and thirty-one I held twelve different full-time jobs in construction, heavy manufacturing, electrical maintenance, auto parts sales, rebuilding motors, shoe sales, chemical manufacturing, securities, and as a WTMJ FM-radio engineer (a silent disc jockey). I did not remain in any one of these positions for any duration because they either paid very little money, were temporary, were eliminated, the business closed or I was unsuited for the work. I tried hard to find an industry where I felt I belonged, but I made little progress.

In 1953, at the age of thirty-one, I was accepted for life insurance sales at the Willard (Bill) L. Momsen Agency of Northwestern Mutual. My previous sales experience and the results of a Strong interest test that the Momsen Agency gave me indicated that I should make a good sales agent. At this time I had a wife and young child.

It was an impressive place to work and learn. There were many successful agents in the office and Northwestern Mutual Life (the quiet company) was and still is the premier life insurance company.

At the end of six months I was a classic failure and an embarrassment to Bill Momsen, the general agent. When Bill called me into his office I knew what was going to happen. The gentleman he was, he tried to let me down easily. He said I did not have a prayer of making it as a successful life insurance salesman.

Bill sincerely wanted to help. He suggested I see Dr. Paul Mundie, an occupational psychologist, who could help me find another job quickly. As it was, during this six month period I had borrowed money to support my family and I needed immediate income.

After a week of meeting with Dr. Mundie and taking a number of tests he indicated I might succeed in the drywall construction industry. He explained, "this was a business where, after some experience in drywall installation, you could go out on your own with very little capital. And your previous sales experience would help."

"What other occupations do the tests show?" I asked.

"There are other interest areas, such as engineering and the ministry, but they require a college education. With your educational background and immediate financial need these do not appear to be an alternative," Dr. Mundie replied.

"Anything else?"

"The life insurance profession is fairly high on the test," he admitted, "but you failed at that, so we can rule it out."

"What can there be about life insurance that it recommends?" I pursued. "Calling on strangers to buy life insurance, being rejected and insuring people in case they die does not appeal to me."

"Maybe that is why life insurance sales is not for you," Dr. Mundie agreed. "Since you are currently operating independently in life insurance sales, the test indicated you may be entrepreneurial and want to be your own boss; and, for that same reason, the test may have shown life insurance sales as an interest. Tests tell us more of what we think we like to do than what abilities we have." He showed me the results of my Strong test and explained how to interpret it, I found it fascinating. "This is an interest test," he explained, "a comparative test to other successful people in certain occupations, not a test that shows what abilities you have."

I was still impressed and the test results continued to trouble me. If the test showed I could succeed at life insurance sales, maybe I could. Every job has its difficult parts, and I didn't know if my self confidence could survive another job change and possible failure.

I told Bill how I felt about the company and the other agents in the agency, and that this is where I needed to make a stand. He shook his head and said, "Don, people who fail as you have don't make it. It takes a certain kind of person to succeed in life insurance and you're evidently not it."

"But the tests say I can succeed. I am not going to fail. I need to try again," I insisted.

"Don, you're doing the wrong thing. You're going deeper in debt and your confidence is low. It's a bad combination."

I kept at him for a few days and must have been convincing. Finally, Bill agreed. "All right, six months more. If you are not making it by then you have to agree to no more arguments, that will be the end. And, no financial help. You are completely on your own."

Two years later at the annual agency dinner Bill Momsen presented me with the coveted Top Agency Award. It was quite an emotional experience for my wife Donna and me— and Bill Momsen too.

Seven years later I had every life insurance industry award hanging on my office walls, including the prestigious Million Dollar Round Table Award. And, after six years of night courses at the University of Wisconsin, Milwaukee, (in spite of the fact I barely made it through high school) I received a Certified Life Insurance Underwriters (C.L.U.) degree. The Strong test I had taken for Dr. Mundie so long ago had quite an affect on me.

Life insurance was very hard and demanding work, and to accomplish these objectives I had to work and study many twelve-hour days and seven-day weeks. In addition to life insurance sales I was asked to teach insurance at the Milwaukee vocational and adult school three nights a week. I did this teaching for three years and found it enjoyable. Although I was now successful, I still found some areas of life insurance sales went against my nature.

As a member of the Million Dollar Round Table (MDRT) I attended national meetings with agents from other life insurance companies. During these week-long business meetings I would meet hundreds of the most powerful and capable sales people at the time. These were mavericks, just like me, who needed freedom to use their abilities in their own way and to control their own destiny. I doubted that any of them had chosen life insurance; life insurance had chosen them.

These highly-talented MDRT members came from all walks of life. Many were former doctors, lawyers, accountants and bankers. All of them had one thing in common: they were ordinary people who found the freedom and opportunity in the life insurance environment to use their talents. There was nothing exceptional about these people—except they had found the means and the environment to become special. Each individual used his or her talents differently. No two agents applied themselves to life insurance sales in the same way. They were the most unlikely looking group of successful people I had seen anywhere.

It occurred to me that if this group of Million Dollar Round Table sales people could be successful, then perhaps anyone given a free environment to find and use his or her talents could become successful. Was this the start of my belief that many people may have undiscovered talent that could be found if allowed the freedom and opportunity?

After my success in life insurance sales I became a believer in the value of interest testing. As an agent I ran interest tests on clients and potential clients who had career problems. Later, when I started companies of my own I used interest tests while interviewing job applicants.

In 1969, through an unusual twist of fate, I became an investor in Marine Biochemists, a small start-up partnership in the surface water treatment field. After a few years the company was failing. My signature was on their bank note, so I had to became involved to try and save the company and to prevent its notes from being called in by the lender. With my sales help the company started to experience some success and I found owning and running a business more to my liking than life insurance sales. I ultimately left the agency.

In 1970 I formed a second company, Applied Biochemists, Inc. with world-wide manufacturing and selling rights accept for the state of Wisconsin that remained with Marine Biochemists. Ultimately I bought out the remaining Marine Biochemists partner.

By 1985, Applied Biochemist had offices and distributors established across the U.S.A. and abroad. We developed over thirty new products and I was the initiator and co-author of new chemical patents that became the core of the business.

The experience of working with many different companies as a business and estate insurance advisor was a great help. From one small company and borrowed capital a conglomerate of companies was created. We developed, manufactured and had our own staff selling lake, pond, swimming pool and waste water chemicals. In addition to the main company, we had a mail order company, an enzyme company, and a company that treated lakes and ponds in Wisconsin, with branches in California, Arizona and Texas.

Throughout the 1970s and 1980s I used the same Strong interest test when interviewing sales and technical people in almost every major city in the United States. Although only one out of fifty applicants was hired, I attempted to assist everyone I interviewed by reviewing the interests their tests indicated and encouraging them to consider those interests and education.

As I observed and counseled thousands of individuals, I developed a theory that companies are not built by people but rather by the talents of people. I became increasingly interested in talent, especially sales talent.

Most of our employees were sales people. In our business we were attempting to sell products that no one had ever heard of before. The difficulty was in finding someone who could be successful at and enjoy the repetitious selling of our products by building a dealer and distributor network in the field. We also had a telemarketing sales staff in the home office. In the beginning the turn over in our sales departments was very high as they were required to build distribution in four different markets: surface water, fisheries, and swimming pools and waste water. They had to work with, educate and trouble shoot problems for distributors, dealers and end users, including, government agencies, municipalities and commercial firms.

Over the years I retained the thousands of Strong tests from all those I interviewed including the sales people we hired, both successful and unsuccessful . By comparing the average Strong test interests of our successful and unsuccessful sales people a certain combination of occupational interests for successful sales people for our company became apparent. One would have thought that a test of an individual high in merchandising and sales, as found in the

Strong enterprising theme, would indicate a potential success. This did not prove to be true. What became obvious was that although the successful sales people rated very high in sales and merchandising on the Strong test they also showed: the aggressiveness and command presence of military and police officers; the dedication and competitiveness of athletes; the vocalization opportunity of public speaking, law and politics; an interest in people, as in teaching and recreation professions; the sincerity and honesty of the ministry; and adventure, as in being out in the field on their own with the challenge of meeting new people in different environments.

The applicants did not have to rate extremely high in all of these areas, but they could not be less than average in more than one or two. This resulted in an unusual but logical profile consisting of a combination of interests necessary for a person to succeed at selling our products.

The "Select Profile System" consisted of taking parts of professions an individual had interests in, rather than the professions themselves and combining those parts into a profile to identify the kind of sales person we needed. The "Select Profile System" may not have been a completely new approach but it is highly dependent upon the skill and interest of the person conducting the profile.

I continued to improve the profile and used it in selecting people for our sales staff, eventually lowering the turn over rate of the sales departments. In later years our sales staff was the envy of our industry, including competitors in the Fortune 500. By maintaining an environment that our sales staff needed and enjoyed, they returned peak performances, loyalty and dedication.

At the age of sixty-eight I chose to change careers again, for a quieter career where I could enjoy completing some of the books I had started over the years; so, in 1989 we sold the companies to a British conglomerate who wanted the companies we had built. Although I had stories to complete, "talent" continued to invade my thoughts . . . and even my story lines.

I tried to define this interest in talent and in doing so, asked myself: "Was it talent I was trying to uncover or was it simply a method of identifying and selecting people who fit into a particular occupation niche? My interest seemed to stem from the belief that workers and students desperately needed an acceptable method of choosing careers and courses of study that meshed with their capabilities. In fact, everyone does. In addition, since there is no method available to discover a person's capabilities or talents, our system of public education cannot educate according to individual capability as it should.

It further occurred to me that with my limited education I was an example of someone who should not have succeeded. Luckily, in my exposure to so many industries I must have uncovered some talents and capabilities; and, because I had the freedom and environment to use my talents, I succeeded.

I further suspected that if I could succeed, with my poor scholastic school performance, then most anyone could . . . if they found some of their hidden talents supported by a strong desire to succeed.

I never forgot the Strong test I took, and the confidence it gave me to believe I could succeed at life insurance sales. There was power in interest test results that can inspire confidence, change lives and reverse failures. Although Dr. Mundie told me few test results are occupational dependable, I was strongly impressed with the test results that somehow worked well for me and the "Select Profile System" that was developed through the years from the tests.

Strangely enough, I found out that employers and personnel people became hesitant to use such tests. The landmark 1971 ruling, Griggs V. Duke Power Co., prohibits business from using what they call mental tests unless they could prove the test had a "manifest relationship to the employment in question."

I used these tests as a starting point of the interview rather than a tool to eliminate people from jobs; and I tried to help all applicants in their job search and career goals.

I asked career professionals if they were familiar with the Strong test. Some knew of it and said interest tests were helpful; others were not impressed. I talked with teachers who used Strong and other tests; they thought these tests were helpful but were not overly enthusiastic. How could this be? Why were others not as impressed as I? Something was wrong. Why did it work for me and not for other people? I may have been overreacting. I decided to find out more about these tests.

4

Margo - a Case Study
July 1968

*Your mission here on earth is one which is
uniquely yours, to exercise that talent which you
particularly came to earth to use-your greatest gift.*
RICHARD NELSON BOLLES,
WHAT COLOR IS YOUR PARACHUTE?

People who have not been exposed to career counseling may
wonder how the test counseling process works. My experience with interest testing started forty years ago with the
use of the Strong Campbell Interest Inventory, later called Strong
Campbell Interest Blank. Interest testing is of value in career counseling. Presently, career and psychological tests are the only career
assessment tools that are utilized.

No two individuals are counseled the same. The counselor analyzes the test results and has the individual contemplate interest-
suggested occupations. The individual's answers and comments to
such occupations lead the counseling. The counselor is only a guide;
other than an employment application and test information the
counselor knows nothing about the individual. On the other hand
the individual knows everything about him/herself, most of which
they are not consciously aware.

I believe a career counselor's objective is to help the person taking the test help themselves, so the person taking the test believes any conclusions drawn are their ideas rather than the counselor's. I usually knew at the end of the interview if my efforts to help the individual fell on fertile ground. After a counseling session I seldom heard if or how an individual used my help. The following case is an example of one person I counseled and later did hear from.

This story will make my search for a talent discovery concept easier to understand. The young woman that I came in contact with demonstrates how my approach to career and job counseling based on interest testing may work.

One day when our company was holding job interviews, I entered the lobby and spotted a young woman seated there. She was looking rather apprehensive and failed to look up as I walked into the room. (Usually an applicant is aware of someone entering the lobby from the office.) Her failure to look up and the way she gazed out the window made me stop. I asked my secretary if the woman was here for a job interview. I was told that she was waiting to be interviewed.

Whenever possible I tried to personally interview all job applicants. I would even attempt to help the individuals who were not hired, by giving them an "interest test" and suggesting they investigate jobs more compatible with their occupational interests.

I asked our personnel manager if the young woman qualified for the job. "No," he said, "we have applicants who are better qualified." I asked him for her file. After I reviewed it I asked my secretary to show the young woman into my office.

The young woman ushered into my office was about five-feet seven-inches tall and slightly overweight. She had shoulder-length dark brown hair that was draped around her shoulders, with bangs across her forehead. She had a gypsy look: clear pearl complexion; high cheek bones; dark eyes; soft features; and white, even teeth. Her face had character; a little puffy but attractive.

She was evidently uncomfortable in her solid dark skirt that was obviously too small (perhaps caused by a recent weight gain resulting from her job frustration). She wore a neat, white blouse with a lace collar underneath a black, open-knit shawl with long fringes. She appeared ill at ease, sitting on the edge of the chair as if she would leave quickly when she was turned down for the job (as she appeared to expect).

Her employment application indicated she was single and lived in a rooming house on Milwaukee's east side. She had attended high school in Chicago, and was a second year liberal arts college dropout. She had held three waitress jobs while in college, and four jobs since leaving college: two clerical, one production line in a printing firm, and one waitress position. Her reasons for leaving these positions were typical: one company cut back, one closed down, and two she left to better herself.

Her name was Margo. (This is not her real name but she looked like a Margo. Since interviews are confidential, I cannot use real names.) After some small talk, I began our conversation.

"Margo, if I may call you that?" She smiled and nodded. "If I were to offer you any job in the world at a good salary, what would it be?"

The opening question surprised her. She shook her head, her eyes went back and forth, and then she shrugged. "I don't really know . . . something in an office, I guess."

"Let me ask the question in a different way. Have you ever had a dream in which you were doing some enjoyable work or had a position you really liked?"

Another strange question. She frowned, then placed her hands together under her chin and looked away. "Well . . . but it's a little . . . " She shook her head. "Oh it's ridiculous, it could never be."

"I would be complimented if you told me, no matter how impossible it may sound." She was apparently trying to figure out what this had to do with the job. Finally she decided to go along.

As she spoke, she gazed through the window behind my desk. "I had this dream a few times, we.̈ . . . . maybe more than a few times, that I owned a company . . . with many people." She spoke so softly I could barely hear her. "And, I had a beautiful office overlooking a park with water . . . and everyone was respectful and nice to me, because I was very successful and talented. I had my own secretary. And, I had a beautiful apartment that I furnished myself . . . I was invited to cocktail parties . . . and I dressed very nicely in designer clothes." With that she stopped talking, dropped her hands to her side and pushed herself up a little. She did not look at me to see my reaction.

I was silent. Remaining silent was very difficult but I needed to know her next comments. Finally Margo could stand the silence no longer. In a somewhat brassy tone she said: "Well, you asked and I told you." She spread her hands and looked down at herself. "Well, look at me. How could I ever do or be someone like that?"

I was still silent. She went on "It's just a dream. I could never do it."

Finally, I smiled. "Of course you can, and many people have. It happens every day. What is there to prevent you? Someone is going to be in that office you dream about. Why not you?"

She sat back in her chair, shook her head slightly and saw the quizzical look on my face. "Oh no, you're not going to give me that 'I can move mountains' thing." I did not respond. "You think I can really do it, huh? Don't you? Hah, then everyone would be able to do it, and you know what the chances of that are."

"I'm not concerned about anyone else right now," I said, "just you and your dream. Let me tell you something about myself. I had nothing when I started. I used to bicycle through a suburb just north of Milwaukee and look at all the beautiful homes situated on wooded acres of land owned by wealthy families. It was way beyond my wildest dreams to own a home in that area. Today I own a home in that area."

"Sure, but you must have had help from your parents . . . or an education or something."

"My stepfather was a truck driver and my mother was a waitress. They wanted me to learn a trade, like a shoemaker or a butcher. It took me an extra semester to graduate from grade and high school."

She thought about what I had said, and put her hands under chin again (evidently her thinking mode). Finally she said. "I'm not going to get the job, am I?"

"No."

"I'm not qualified, huh?"

"Let's just say there are others more qualified than you."

She nodded. I could tell what her thoughts were: "Well if I don't have the job, what does this old guy want from me? Why all of these questions? Oh, oh, I'd better be careful."

At this point Margo began to look around my office in an attempt to learn where I was coming from. Maybe she could find something in the room to give her a hint. On the wall behind my desk were four framed, silver Franklin Mint plates. One was of Paul Revere alerting the colonists, a second one was a colonists' Thanksgiving scene, the third was of the signing of the Declaration of Independence, and the final one was of Christ's Resurrection. She studied these plates for a moment. They seemed to reassure her that I was okay. She looked back at me.

I continued. "My home is surrounded by forest. There is a pond, a swimming pool, two Siamese cats and I have a wonderful wife who understands me."

She laughed, shrugged and sat back as if to say, 'okay, what now?'

"If I can do it, you can do it," I said. "A person can make their dreams come true if they want to badly enough. You have to become a student at finding out what your best abilities are. You will need to work hard, volunteer, get a lot of exposure, set short-term goals for yourself, and make overcoming obstacles a game. To keep your dream alive, repeat your dream to yourself every day and in your prayers every night. To do this you have to have a plan."

Now she appeared more relaxed and open. The job was gone.

"Sure, it's easy for you. You're one of the lucky ones. I don't know what I'm good at and I'm not very lucky."

"There were more ulcers than luck. I just wouldn't quit, although I thought about it many sleepless nights."

"Well, maybe you're more motivated or something."

"I don't believe God gave one person more motivation energy than another." She said nothing. "So your dream means nothing?"

She seemed uncomfortable and adjusted herself in her chair again, and took a deep breath, letting out a big sigh. "Yes, it means something." She rubbed her hands together and looked down. When she looked up again her eyes were glassy. "Yes . . . it does." She sniffed and wiped her eyes. "But I can't even get a job to support myself. I'm on the dole. Every time I have to go down to that stinking place and stand in line for my unemployment check . . . do you know how degrading that is?" she asked vehemently.

I didn't answer, but I knew how it was. Even though we didn't have an unemployment office or unemployment checks when I was young and out of work, I could understand. She sobbed and took out a tissue. "I'm sorry, I don't mean to throw my problems at you, but darn it, it's hard and it's humiliating." Sniff. "But, you asked."

I was silent.

She swallowed to hold back the tears. Now I knew what she really was: a sincere and frightened young woman with no place to go and no one to turn to for help. She would get another job in some backwater place, afraid to ask for a raise or to leave and better herself. The job would become boring, frustrating and unsatisfying to the point that it hurt. She would spend the rest of her life dreading going to work in the morning. Her nights and weekends would be spent in the wrong places with the wrong people.

She sighed, picked up her purse and started to rise. "Maybe I can help," I said. "Let's talk about your job future." She did not object and sat back down in the chair.

I told her I sympathized with her problems and I understood how difficult they must be to contend with. Although she did not qualify for our position I explained I was willing to try to help her find an occupational direction which perhaps was more suited to her interests.

I asked her if she had ever taken a career or interest test in school. Yes, she had taken a vocational guidance test in high school to establish college direction. The counselor told her she should be a travel agent or a beautician. (Almost every female tests high in those two vocations. It is more an indication of someone who would like to look nice, travel and get away from problems rather than a true vocational interest.) Margo had not taken a career test in college.

I suggested that she take a Strong test. I would send the test in for analysis (the Strong test was sent to California or Minneapolis and a computerized form was returned that showed interest suggestions that the counselor could analyze and use in the follow-up interview), and then we might find some career clues for her.

Margo said she would be interested in the results and thanked me for the help. After drying her eyes, she apologized for taking up my time with her problems. Although she may have felt a little better after unburdening her problems on someone, the hopelessness was still visible in her walk as she left. I turned Margo over to my secretary so that she could take the Strong test. I did not expect to see Margo again as most people do not return to a place where they were rejected for a job.

Margo Comes Back

I had forgotten about Margo until my secretary informed me that Margo's test results had come back. I took the test home with me and spent an hour analyzing it that evening. I saw a well-supported interest cluster for a potential vocation direction that might fit her dream. That was not unusual. A test can be an expression of an individual's dream. I studied her interest in positive occupations and negative or low scoring occupations and their relationship with each other. I went back into the question sheet for conflicts, with suggested occupations. The test result had possibilities. I was encouraged. This young woman was crying for any kind of help.

I personally telephoned Margo and encouraged her to come in for the test results. She was somewhat cool, said she would consider it and call me back. To my surprise she called my secretary for an appointment and came in the next day. Margo came in wearing the same clothes and the best face-saving smile she could put on. Her body language indicated suspicion and uncertainty as to why I was bothering with her.

"Your test appears to have something of value," I began, "but before we start I would like to know a little more about your family." I wanted to learn how much family support she could rely on.

Margo was an only child. Her mother worked at the telephone company and divorced her husband ten years ago. Margo's father was a foundry worker who evidently drank too much at times. There was something else in the father-daughter relationship, a coolness, a resentment. There were indications of mother-daughter confrontations. The mother was disappointed that Margo had constant school and job problems. Margo said she didn't blame her mother, since it seemed that Margo made wrong decisions and did all the wrong things. There was an indication of affection for her mother.

"Margo, whose fault is it that you are without a job?"

"They were cutting back." (The company probably told her to say this.) Then she shrugged and with a sigh said: "Oh hell, if you want the truth, probably mine. I just can't seem to settle down. I get so bored with routine jobs and the other girls sense it. I don't develop lasting friends."

I came around from behind my desk and sat in the companion arm chair in front of my desk. She swiveled her chair to face me. I usually hesitated to lead a person towards a specific occupation but with her low self esteem and high failure rate I needed to develop a definite target so Margo would be interested enough to commit to some form of action. (An individual such as Margo becomes discouraged easily.)

"Margo, I want to tell you a story. Do you have a few minutes?"

She shrugged her shoulders. "I'm here. Sure. Why not?"

"In this story, there's a lovely woman in her sixties who looks much younger than her years. She is beautifully dressed, with carefully styled hair and expensive but tasteful jewelry. This is a dinner party at a private club in a large city. Along side this lady are her adult children, an equally well-groomed daughter and professional looking son. The others in attendance are people she has worked with for years: employees and their husbands and wives, business associates, bankers, lawyers and accountants. There are even business competitors in attendance. Everyone has come to honor this lady. We can tell that she is well-respected and loved by these people. It's a retirement party. The woman is transferring the helm of her company to the capable hands of her daughter, so she can spend time in her home in Connecticut, where she wants to do some painting, writing and relaxed traveling. Perhaps she will even be a guest lecturer at a girl's college, as she has been asked.

"It was a difficult decision to give up the helm of her company but she will still be chairman of the board. It's time to turn the business over to her daughter, who is also well-respected in the firm. Her son is a lawyer in a well-known law firm.

"Her successful career is now almost over. She has gone as high as she can go. It is not sad. Her friends will still be her friends. She can continue to watch her daughter grow. They can have long lunches and discuss how things are going. So why not get off at the top? She has done it all. Perhaps there are new, less stressful challenges."

I had Margo's complete attention. She smiled quietly, a little glassy-eyed. "Tell me how you feel about that story, Margo."

She blinked, swallowed. "Oh." She sighed. "Lucky woman."

"It's not a true story, Margo; but it is a story that can come true forty years from now. You can be that woman."

Tears came to her eyes. She sniffed and looked up. "That's a low blow . . . you use a person's dream . . . ?"

I didn't respond to that. "Let's carry this one step further Margo. Let's say that forty years from now I am invited to this party. You come up to me and tell me that you were glad I came. I would ask you this question: 'Looking back I'm sure you loved all the growing years of your company. What I want to know Margo is this: how difficult was it?' Now Margo picture yourself forty years from now. Your daughter, son, associates and friends are all gathered to honor you. How would you answer me? Think carefully before you answer. How difficult was it?"

She swiveled around slowly and looked out the window behind my desk. A minute must have passed. She turned back to me and frowned. "I don't really know how to answer that . . . but . . . well . . . I guess it was tough in the beginning." Then with a soft smile. She said. ". . . but it was fun." She looked out the window again for a few moments, shrugged her shoulder and pursed her lips. "Oh heck . . . I guess looking back it really couldn't have been so difficult after all."

I nodded. I could see the wheels spinning in her head as she digested what she had said. She frowned a little and put her thumb nail to her lower lip, nodded her head slightly and turned back to me. "You really think I can do that, don't you?"

"I don't know if you will, but I believe you can."

She put her hand up to her mouth again. Her hand was trembling a little. Then softly she said, "How can I do that? See how I look? I don't have any talent." Then with a sob, "I don't even know what I want to do. I don't even have a job." Tears came to her eyes; they no longer embarrassed her in front of me, a sign of openness and trust.

"Do you have any other special interests we haven't talked about?"

She sighed and dried her eyes with a tissue. "No, that's why I couldn't make it in college. I didn't know what I wanted to study. I couldn't go on . . . what a waste. It's going to take me years to pay off my student loan as it is, and they're after me now because I'm behind in payments."

"We all go through these problems, Margo. Let's see if we can find a way to help."

Developing a Plan

Now, with the aid of the test information, I started asking questions. "You must have some interests. Do you draw or paint?"

"Well, I used to sketch dresses and women's clothing."

"Were they any good?"

"Well, I thought the designs were okay but the figure drawings weren't so hot."

"Did you take any art courses?"

"No. I can't draw."

"They can improve your figure drawing and a lot of successful designers can't draw. Could you picture yourself developing promotional ideas at an advertising agency?"

"Oh sure. There are a thousand girls with degrees who would like to do that. The competition is fierce."

"What are you going to do now?"

"Keep looking for a new job," she said wistfully. "Hopefully one that isn't boring," she added resignedly with a shrug. I was starting to lose her again.

"Margo, I want you to listen carefully to what I have to say. You are a very special person; in fact you are wonderful. The good Lord only made one of you. He created you because He has a special purpose for you; something only you can do. He gave you the ability to accomplish it. If you don't find that ability and use it, his creation of you is wasted. He is not going to tell you what He wants you to do in neon lights nor will He speak to you in a voice of thunder. He gave you a good brain, a body and all of the equipment you need. That is as far as He can go. The rest is up to you."

Margo sat upright. I let her think for a moment. She was going to have to talk because I was not. Finally, in a quiet voice she said, "You think I'm wonderful?"

"I think you are ever so wonderful."

"You really think God cares about me?"

"Why else would He place you here?"

"He placed lots of people here."

"Yes, and every one is special."

She looked at me. Should she believe I was sincere in saying she was wonderful and had a purpose; or was I saying it for a reason? Margo evidently decided to trust me. She folded her hands, looked at me, and said quietly, "What should I do?"

"It's not up to me," I gently replied. "What are you going to do?"

"I want to do something so badly . . . that's the problem. I don't know what to do." No shrugs or brazenness anymore. I thought I could work with her now. I sensed a sincere young woman under that facade, a potentially valuable person. She would be worth the time and effort.

"Perhaps we can help you find a direction. No promises, okay? Let's see what we can do." She nodded.

Margo's test results showed a nice cluster of interests. She came across as being introverted but in her situation this could be temporary. A possible self starter, she tested high in investigative and enterprising areas. Some bands of occupational test scores were very negative but that could also change. Margo was just down now. When a person taking the test is down it can influence and depress their scores, thereby slanting the test results. I had learned not to take tests at face value. Sometimes low occupation scores held more clues than high scores. There was often another painting under the one you saw.

"You evidently had difficulty adjusting to certain school subjects?" I asked.

"That's true, most were boring. But the things I liked a lot I could really dig into."

"Your test shows a medium- to strong-sized cluster of art, writing, secretarial, advertising, public relations and broadcasting."

"Cluster?"

"A group of occupations that can exist under the same roof or the same business area. In your situation, advertising is the industry which utilizes all of those interests."

"That's good, huh?"

"It could be, but interest does not indicate capability."

She frowned. "Oh. Capability?"

"It means you may like or prefer those occupations but you may not be talented enough to hold or succeed in them. Tests indicate interests not talents."

"Oh. So what good are the tests?"

"They give us a starting point, something to talk about, something to think about and for you to research. Your interest cluster matches your dream, and this may rightly or wrongly provide you with the motivation to pursue this interest. At least the cluster gives us a basis to explore."

"Does everyone's dream match their cluster?"

"It is not common from my experience."

She sat up. "That is good, isn't it?"

"We really do not know."

"Oh." Again disappointed, she sat back.

"There are some interests we could explore. As an example, you show interest as a military officer; which could be an indication of a desire to be a leader or to command others. The strengths you show in other positions (personnel director, teacher and guidance counselor) may indicate interests in working with and helping other people or employees. Your ministry strength may indicate honesty and sincerity. Athletic strength may indicate competitiveness."

"You can tell all that from a test?"

"Possibly, but we don't know your level of capability in some of these areas." I started opening doors to Margo's cluster occupations by asking her questions about what she saw.

"Margo, how do you feel about writing?"

"I'm not good at it; but I like to write. I have a good imagination, I think."

"What kind of things do you write?"

"Oh, stories and poems and things; nothing worthwhile."

"I notice from your application you type well and know shorthand. Have you thought of secretarial work?"

"I like to type but I get bored typing the same things over and over again. My shorthand is weak. I would be afraid to attempt secretarial. I make too many mistakes."

"I'm sure experience and confidence will take care of mistakes. Would you feel comfortable working in television?"

"Yes, that sounds interesting."

"Would you be more comfortable acting, reporting, directing shows, or developing and writing TV shows."

"Writing and developing shows . . . and directing would be fun . . . women's advertising . . . fashion shows I would like."

"Would you be more comfortable developing an ad for TV or presenting an advertising program to a client?"

"I don't know. I'm not good in front of people but I do like to develop ideas. I could do better than some of those dumb TV ads I've seen." With my questions she was closing in on what I saw as a possible entry to her interest cluster. It is not often you can become this specific.

The Plan

"Let's see what we can put together from your test and comments," I suggested. "Advertising is the anchor of your interests. A position as a private secretary would be an entry into the industry. As a private secretary to the president of an advertising agency you could watch, listen and learn the advertising business firsthand at a high level, where the real decisions are made. You would gather experience and knowledge, and perhaps you would have the opportunity to design, develop, write and express your ideas. If not, change to a company where you can express yourself. Continue to observe and learn the industry. Then, with top knowledge and experience you could start a business of your own. How do you feel about that?"

She sat there looking at me with her mouth open. "Oh wow . . . private secretary to an advertising agency president, where I could learn and do all of those things? Design and develop . . . a business of my own." She took out a pad and evidently wrote the plan down. She looked up at me with wonder in her eyes. It was as if someone had opened a whole new world for her. She said, "Why didn't I think of this? Or perhaps I have in a hazy way or at least it seems familiar . . . or something I never thought I could do. It all seems to fit . . . makes so much sense. It's . . . it's w-wonderful . . . a plan. I never had a real plan before."

Then it started to dawn on her again, as I knew it would. How could she possibly attain a position like that? In her mind it was beyond anything she could ever do or qualify for. "It is a wonderful dream. But—look at me." She spread her hands and looked down at herself. "Do I look like an efficient secretary . . . and my poor education and experience. How could I ever qualify to do that?"

"Can't you change your appearance and get more experience?"

"Well, maybe."

"Would you want to change the plan in any way?"

"No."

"It's a reasonable plan that seems to fit. Have you any other plan or better ideas?"

"No, but . . . well . . . what makes you think I can do all this?"

"I have many years of experience working with and watching people fail and succeed."

"And you think I can do it?"

"It is possible, especially if you muster the inner strength to start and find the will power you will need to keep going. You appear to have a strong desire."

"Huh." She shook her head and looked me straight in the eyes. "I guess you ought to know. I don't see what you have to gain by saying so . . . well, okay. Let's go for it!" She put her hand to the side of her face, looked down and around, then shook her head from side to side. "I don't know how. What do I do now?"

"We develop a first stage action plan. If you agree to it, then you do it."

"That's all, huh? Just like that and it's done, right?" She shook her head. "Wow!" She looked at me again. I could see her brain was working. Finally she said, "You realize all the things I have to do to accomplish this? Have you taken a good look at me? Can you imagine me as a secretary to the president of an advertising agency?" She sighed. "But, so what? If you think I can do it . . ." Again I said nothing. "Where do I start?"

"First I am going to make some unusual and necessary suggestions to give you the best chance of success. Promise me you won't be insulted at my suggestions."

"Suggestions?" She frowned. "W-w-well, like what?"

"Take a Dale Carnegie course."

"A what? Oh, I've heard of that, a kind of confidence-building thing. I guess I'm going to need that; but, that costs money."

"You're not working now. You have the time. Go to them and offer to lick stamps, stuff envelopes, make telephone sales calls, whatever they need in exchange for free tuition. Carnegie is a great confidence builder, it helps you come out of your shell. You will also meet many kinds of people in different situations. You'll realize we are all alike. You will have a chance to share your dream with other people who have dreams like yours. If you're lucky, you will make friends who will take an interest in your plan and you will make each other account for your progress. You will need all of the help and confidence you can muster to proceed."

"Okay. I'll try it. What's next?"

"Take a modeling course."

She burst out laughing. "You're serious . . . a modeling course? What for? Look at me I couldn't be a model if I wanted to. Oh! They make you lose weight. You want me to lose weight, right?"

"Plain Jane's take modeling courses too. Don't sell yourself short. I don't think there is any question you can be a very impressive and attractive young woman. Every woman should take a modeling and grooming course; they owe it to themselves and the rest of the world to present what God gave them in the best light. It is especially important in the advertising business, since that industry is very conscious of grooming. How you look and present yourself can make the difference between doors opening or shutting for you."

"I would feel a little funny going there, but I see what you mean. How do I pay for this?"

"When business conventions are in town agencies need part-time help during the day and on weekends. Ask at the modeling agencies. Get some experience and your name on the agency convention lists. Use your ingenuity."

"I would have to lose weight fast. What about the clothes? That takes money."

"Used clothes outlets have great dresses worn only once."

"Money?"

"Offer to work part-time for minimum wage or for a few outfits if you have to. They often need help to fill-in, especially at night and on weekends. Being there, you could get first choice of the clothes coming in."

She laughed. "You make it sound so easy and simple."

"It isn't. These are only ideas and suggestions; and they may not work. It's up to you to find a way. You will have to start taking day or evening courses in secretarial skills, like shorthand and computers. And then, as you can, in commercial art, advertising, marketing, promotion and writing."

After hearing all of this, she sat back and took a deep breath.

"Computers, marketing, promotion? Oh I see, those are all a part of it, right?"

"Knowledge is what you need. You are going to have to work to support yourself. In the beginning concentrate on finding an office job in a small advertising agency or two for exposure. Offer to be on call for when they need someone. They may need a temporary model. In time you will be trained, capable and competent. When you're ready, make appointments with every advertising agency president who will talk with you. Tell them you want to be their secretary and you will be the best secretary they ever had. Tell them your dream. Eventually one of the agencies will need a secretary or you may sell yourself into some other temporary or responsible position. The plan is not fixed. If a door opens that offers you opportunity to move up down or sideways to get additional experience then do it. Don't be afraid to move. Keep sight of your goal. Does that plan fit what you feel you need?"

"Yes it does. I know it is going to take time, but you have me believing I can do it. Oh, I'm excited now; but will it last? Do you really believe I can do it?"

"What other choice do you have? Do you have a better plan to solve the heavy load of problems you carry on your back every day?"

"No."

The Getting to Know You Exercise

"Margo, all I can do is help you develop a plan. Since we have no way of discovering ability or talents in people, I don't know what hidden talents you may have in some other field. Maybe you have the ability to be a great brain surgeon or a renowned chemist. I have no way of knowing. However, I do have a method to help you know yourself better. I call it the "Getting to Know You" exercise. Here's what I want you to do.

"I have circled certain occupations on this test. Take it with a pad of paper to the public library. Look up each of the occupations your test suggests in The U.S. Department of Labor *Dictionary of Occupations* or the *1988-89 Occupational Handbook*. Some of these occupations will be listed in these reference manuals and some won't; you may have to search in other books for them.

"Under each occupation they list the job tasks involved in that specific occupation. Make a page for each of these occupations and draw three lines down the page, separating the page into four columns. At the top of the page, write the name of the occupation, such as secretary. At the top of the first column write 'job tasks,' at

Getting To Know You Exercise

SECRETARY

Job Tasks	Like	Indifferent	Dislike
Schedule appointments	X		
Give information to callers	X		
Organize and maintain files		X	
Fill out forms			X
Take and transcribe dictation	X		
Routing mail		X	
Answering telephones	X		
Answering letters	X		
Doing research			X
Preparing statistical reports			X
Typing from a recording machine			X
Typing lists of figures			X
Taking down shorthand			X
Keeping up daily appointment book	X		
Breaking appointments			X
Supplying coffee & refreshments			X

the top of the second write 'like,' at the top of the third column write 'indifferent,' and at the top of the fourth column write 'dislike.' In the first column list the secretarial job tasks or activities."

Margo was taking notes as I spoke. She looked up and interrupted. "But Mr. Seymour, I know what I like and dislike about jobs."

"You may think you know your likes and dislikes but when you see them on paper in front of you, and how often certain ones appear, you will be surprised. Write how you feel about each one of those secretarial job tasks. Do the same for each occupation. If you can't find an accurate description of the occupation call and talk with someone who is working in that occupation.

"When you have completed this for all of the occupations, transpose all the job task 'likes' to one page. If a job task 'like' is repeated, write two in front of it; if it is repeated again, then write three. When you have done this, re-write the 'like' list again but this time with the 'likes' most often repeated at the top and on down. Next, repeat this same process with the 'dislikes.' While you are doing this, you will be able to draw your own conclusions.

"Once you have completed this task you will know more about yourself than you ever did before. You will see a most unusual picture unfold, like a photograph suddenly appearing in developing fluid. To succeed you are going to need peak performance from yourself in each one of these occupations."

"It sounds complicated," Margo said, "but I guess it's important. I have to do it. I will."

"Success does not come easily," I continued. "What you are lacking in ability you will need to make up for in effort. People seldom fail doing the things they enjoy; it's the things they don't like that drag them down. Dislikes are your enemy. You must know your enemies well and find the best ways to defeat them."

"You make it sound like a battle."

"It is. Success has a price. That is why most people give up along

the way. We don't want to send you into a battle you are ill prepared to win. With the best knowledge of yourself you have the best
opportunity to maintain control of your direction."

"Wow, this is going to be something." She looked at me for a
few moments and then looked down at what she had written. "It
makes an awful lot of sense. I guess I have to do this; it's the only
hope I have."

"It's a plan and it could change. However, everything you're
going to do will benefit you, no matter what happens or where you
go."

"I know you're right; this is not going to be easy. Why are you
doing this? What do you get out of it?"

"That is not important. Just promise me that you will stay the
course and someday when you make it, find ways to help others
who may need your help."

"When I make it? Oh yes, I promise. Of course I will."

"Repeat your dream each night in a prayer and repeat out loud
your promise to keep working on your plan until you reach your
goal. Remember you are important. You have a purpose. Write this
down. Print it on your bathroom mirror and carry it in your purse.
'When the going gets tough, the tough get going.' " She did.

"Now where are you going to start?"

"I need to get the school curriculums and figure out how many
courses I can afford to take at one time. I need to line up modeling
school and Dale Carnegie, and find work in a used clothing store.
I'll try to get any office job in an advertising agency."

She sat up and said, "Gee it sounds like a lot but it's better than
sitting around worrying and doing nothing. It really doesn't seem
so difficult when I say it . . . but, it's going to take a while. But I'll do
it—somehow."

"One more thing. Forget help wanted ads. Study and select the
advertising company you need to work at to further your plan. Go
see the owner. Tell him or her your dream and how important it is

for you to work there and that you will work harder than anyone else."

"What if the owner won't see me?"

"You won't succeed every time; be persistent. Keep at them. As an owner I would find a way to hire such a dedicated and persistent person, and I have."

She stood up with her head a little higher. "I know you're busy. Thank you." She couldn't raise more than a small, tearful smile before she hurried out of my office.

Margo Leaves

As Margo left my office I thought to myself: to succeed she will have to project a more caring and touching approach to people. She will need the friendship and support of influential people to move up. She will need someone close to answer to; someone who knows her dream and plan. I only hope she will find someone like this. If not, Margo will need strong willpower to follow this plan on her own.

I did not expect to ever hear from Margo again, as I seldom heard from people I had counseled. I knew that I had done my best; but I rarely knew the results of my counseling.

Eight years after Margo walked out my office door I received a telephone call. My secretary said it was "a Margo," who had made a promise to me. I took the call, trying to remember her and to recall the circumstances. (I had counseled so many people through the years that my mind was clouded with a maze of people.) She briefly told me about the plan we had developed for her; the memory came back. I could picture her long, black hair trailing down the open-knit black shawl she had worn over a white lace collar.

Margo said she had been secretary to the president of an advertising agency and had proven to be valuable in developing advertising and promotional campaigns. She had recently been promoted to an account executive for three of the agency's accounts.

"That's wonderful," I remarked.

"I wanted to let you know I am keeping to my goal. I'm not quite there yet; but, now I know I will be. Thank you for your help. On my mirror is still a paper in a plastic cover saying, 'When the going gets tough, the tough get going.' It is also on my vanity mirror, my desk and on my compact mirror. It helped me when I was down many times."

"That is wonderful news. It's so considerate of you to call and let me know your progress."

"I am at the airport and I think my plane is boarding, so I have to go. Again thank you." There was a short period of silence, as though she wanted to say more. Finally, she eked out a "Thank you very much...good-bye."

Several years after this conversation, as I was traveling on a plane to Washington, D.C., I came across a magazine article about "Up and coming women." The picture of one lady caught my eye. There was something familiar about her, The heading referred to her as a successful, upcoming business woman. I looked close at this slim, beautiful woman in a long, black, close-fitting formal. Could that be the Margo who called me a few years ago? The face, the high cheek bones, the eyes, the dark hair, pulled back; they were all vaguely familiar. In the article I found her last name but it was not familiar. It said she was a designer and owner of a fast-growing women's apparel firm. It was so long ago. Could this be Margo? No, it probably was not her, I decided.

A week later I received the same magazine article in the mail, with a handwritten note attached to it:

> *To Mr. Donald Seymour, a very precious gentleman who*
> *unlocked the door for me. I have kept my promise to you.*
> *Thank you sincerely,*
> *Margo*

5

Exposing and Researching Ideas
Spring 1986

In my view, it should be possible to identify an
individual's intellectual profile (or proclivities)
at an early age and then draw upon this knowledge
to enhance that person's educational
opportunities and options.
HOWARD GARDNER, *FRAMES OF MIND*

Margo's case history is an example of the kind of work that can be done when using an individual's interests that have been uncovered by tests. However, we should not be misled by the Margo experience. Tests seldom produce an interest cluster that matches an individual; as it may have for Margo. And, for someone to go the full course, like Margo did, is rare. No matter how hard counselors try to develop a career direction based on someone's interests it is difficult for an individual to seriously pursue a plan if they don't have the ability, talent or the confidence to support it.

Career and interest tests appear to be quite helpful, and they are, but progress is needed before counselors can feel secure in making healthy and efficient career recommendations for individuals. We need more than their interests as a base. Somehow we need to find and qualify an individual's best abilities to support their positive interests. Additionally, we need a way to bypass an individual's misconceptions of what occupations and job tasks entail. Misconceptions can have undue and erroneous influence on an individual's interests, leading to false occupation leads.

Initially I felt good about Margo's note and the article she had sent; but something started to bother me about her situation. Margo's test result cluster could have been a conduit for her dream; subconsciously her test answers slanted in her dream direction. People dream about situations that are attractive and desirable to them but this does not mean it is the right direction for them to follow. In my attempt to help Margo find the best occupation for her, did I place Margo in a stressful environment?

Stress and frustration can result in emotional problems that lead to drug or alcohol abuse, ulcers, heart attacks and cancer. Stress can affect an individual's marriage, resulting in divorce and problems with children. Is Margo subject to any of these ills because her strong, motivated drive for success kept her in a highly-stressed state?

There was no mention of a husband or children. Did her frantic drive for a career end her marriage? Did a stressful career preclude children? If she had sons and daughters how was her relationship with them? Stress can attack the body's most vulnerable organs. Has stress weakened Margo's health and perhaps shortened her life? A goal you dream about and reach may not be the true answer to a successful life.

Could Margo's true calling have been as a chemical oceanographer? The closest the Strong Interest test comes to a chemical oceanographer is a geologist. Her test may have shown geology as a second- or third-level interest without a cluster support, and therefore this occupation was not considered. The Strong test only identifies with eighty-eight common but diversified occupations, geology being one of them.

Furthermore, tests have no way of identifying with the tasks involved in the over 40,000 occupations that exist. Even if chemical oceanographer was one of the eighty-eight occupations on the test, what would Margo know about the work of a chemical oceanographer? Could she have been happier, healthier, more successful and made a great contribution in this field?

When answering questions on career tests, how much does a person know about the daily work both positive and negative involved in the job tasks of the 40,000 estimated occupations? How can a person accurately answer questions about occupations and activities they know little or nothing about? Presently, career search tests are all we have. It is vital to every individual that we improve these tests and design new tools for capability recognition and career selection; especially since a person's occupation may be the most influential part of his/her life.

Working with Students

Can any individual, given wide exposure, opportunity, time and money to pursue specific interests, find a healthful occupation that efficiently fits his/her capabilities? A good question but one that I did not feel qualified to answer. I needed more exposure to different classes and ages of people before I could determine if there was a valid answer.

In 1986, I was introduced to Concordia University in Mequon, Wisconsin (A Missouri Synod Lutheran-sponsored university) by its president, Dr. John Buuck. The university impressed me. I did not expect to meet such dedicated instructors, and to see such cheerful, polite and well-dressed students on a college campus. Courtney Meyer, the Concordia football coach, knew of my business background and asked me to share some of my knowledge with the football team in an effort to guide them on how to succeed in the world of business. In addition to giving each team member a Strong test, I agreed to put on three sessions to the whole team. I also tried to counsel each player individually. It was an interesting experience to work with some of the highest and lowest scholastic students on the campus.

There must have been value in these sessions because the university asked me to take on the responsibility of director of vocational counseling for a year while the director was on a sabbatical. I accepted. This would give me the opportunity to have firsthand experience with college students of various academic levels.

Most students came into my office looking for help in selecting their study major and course direction. Other students felt they were in the wrong major but they did not know what other subject to study. Many of the students did not know there were career search tests available; others had no confidence in these tests.

Even with my experience of counseling thousands of people and conducting thousands of Strong tests, it was difficult to raise interest in some students in any area of their test-suggested occupations. Others were so naive and unexposed to the world of work that their test results provided little information to work with.

Some students even came to see me just before graduation with tears in their eyes. They felt they had chosen the wrong major, and now it was too late to change course. They could not admit their fears to their parents, friends, the university or potential employers. I wondered how many students graduated like this each year.

The next year I worked with students who were attending adult evening classes and working towards a business degree. This was another interesting experience: counseling working adults who were continuing their education. Most of them were enrolled so they could eventually earn more money, get promoted or qualify for a better job. Nothing was wrong with these motivations, except I wanted to hear someone say: "I'm here to find a job more suited to my capabilities."

While I was working at Concordia I also had the opportunity to counsel a few retired people who were referred to me; and this added another dimension to my research.

I soon regretted that I did not have better vocational guidance tools to help the students find their best capabilities, especially the students who, because of indecision or grades, had to drop out of college without finishing their formal education.

One conclusion I started to form at this time was: education and the capability of the student are not necessarily compatible; and education cannot teach according to an individual's capabilities if we have no way of discovering individual capabilities.

The Concordia experience was enlightening, humbling and at times depressing. I knew that my best effort was often of little value to an individual. All I could do was help the person know him or herself better. The problem was how to assist someone make an intelligent decision on their study course or career selection without knowing his/her capabilities? Why has education not committed solid research to the area of finding individual capability?

My experiences at the university confirmed my suspicion that tools for study, career and major selection were badly needed.

Educators know there are problems with our present system. What we need are solutions.

After the Concordia experience I found enjoyment in writing novels; however, I was constantly drawn away from my stories as I continued to draft page after page of my thoughts and ideas on career and talent discovery.

The Riasec School Idea

Education by Attraction is an educational concept I developed: teaching students according to their best interests and wrapping the 3R's around a student's interest area. I called it the Riasec School based upon the six Strong Test General Occupational Themes: realistic, investigative, artistic, social, enterprising and conventional. This was a method of teaching students according to what interested them. Instead of public school as we know it, each student would attend their test-indicated interest school. They could cross over in certain subjects to other school divisions, but their anchor would be their major interest. As they grew and matured their interests might change; then they could easily transfer between the six Riasec divisions with the three R's still in place.

Starting to learn through interest-colored glasses at an early age seemed logical. All students would naturally want to learn in areas that interested them. This should reduce the dropout rate and start career identification at an earlier age. At this time the Riasec school was only an idea to be explored. This raised the question: Is interest a solid foundation for identifying potential capabilities and occupations? At times I had strong doubts about the Riasec interest school; other times I was firmly convinced I had found a better approach to learning and career selection. I knew I had to make a commitment to confirm or deny my beliefs.

In the late 1980s President George Bush set up a New American Schools Committee for the selection and sponsorship of new methods of education. (The Riasec school was a new method of education.) To qualify, a complete school design had to be submitted with an agenda, personnel and budget requirements, etc.

This was more than I could do myself; so, in 1989 I set up and funded a nonprofit foundation, The Vocational Guidance Institute.

The Vocational Guidance Institute

The purpose of the institute was to develop the Riasec school idea and submit it to the New American Schools Committee, and to research, develop and organize other ideas I had developed throughout the years. In addition to the Riasec School, other subjects to be explored were: interest, natural learning, talent discovery, career planning, career adjustment and the effect of careers on life planning, crime, health and marriage.

I rented an office in north Milwaukee. Connie Amos, Michael Puzia, Jory Prosen and Michelle Gagne were hired to do the research and develop the New American Schools design. Connie did some great work on life planning cards and used herself for an example. Jory did special research on the side effects of the Riasec school. Michelle did all the editing. And, with Connie's help, Michael accumulated the Education by Attraction and Riasec ideas into what he called Project Genesis and submitted it to The New American Schools Committee. The model school abstract involved over a hundred pages of support material. The idea must have been too foreign for established educational principles, as it was not selected by the committee.

At the end of two years, the research and school project were completed and we closed the office. The conclusions drawn from our group research indicated that some of the concepts I developed were new, had value and should be pursued. What to do about it now?

I reflected on my life. A wide variety of jobs and varying responsibilities in my business life had given me the opportunity to experience a broad range of activities. From that exposure I found and then developed areas of interest, in highly technical fields for which I was not qualified. My poor performance in school and my resulting business career raised several questions. With my scholastic record, would I have qualified for admission into a college? No.

With my scholastic ability, could I have earned a degree in college? Probably not.

Would I have succeeded in business without the benefit of the wide variety of experiences I had been exposed to? I do not think so.

I exhibited some talent in business and vocational guidance. Why didn't my education bring these interests to the surface? That question was perhaps the start of my belief that if I had capabilities and talents that formal education did not discover then other people may also have hidden abilities.

There are far too many college graduates who upon graduation cannot hold a job in their fields. I know, because when I interviewed applicants I met hundreds of people looking for jobs not in their degrees. After working sporadically in their field of study, many of these college graduates gave up and were working at low paying jobs, some driving taxi cabs or waiting tables. After interviewing and working with these people, I quickly realized far too many individuals have a degree in a profession in which they have no lasting interest, talent or ability. There was no fault to find with the individuals because society has no method of identifying and matching peoples' abilities with occupations. One of our biggest fallacies is that students (and parents) think a person can select a career and then the education system will make each person proficient in their selected field. My experience tells me they are wrong.

Comparing my business history to college graduates who fail in business indicates something is very wrong.

The idea that many people could have hidden talent capability in some unknown area was a substantial departure from established educational principles. Discovering talents not interests should be the focal point of education; so I set the Riasec School idea aside and started to focus on talent discovery.

If we could locate the talents of people, we could educate people according to their talents. Talent would be the pivotal point of education; thereby forcing a change in the way we now educate students to a system that focused on specific group talent education. If people have unknown talents, can we find a "what are we" method of talent discovery?

I hesitated to voice the idea that many people could have undiscovered talent. I felt my peers would think I was daft. I tried to ignore my thoughts. Maybe they would go away. They would not, and new thoughts continued to surface.

Was I on the doorstep to a new science of talent discovery?

6

The Search for Careers
Spring 1987

*Pushing children into activities that do not fit
them as individuals can cause them a great deal of
anger and frustration and can lead to a sorry
waste of their real talents.*
TERESA M. AMABILE, *GROWING UP CREATIVE*

I s not the same true of adults? This is not a book about interest
tests or other career assessment tools used to establish occupational direction. However to understand the need for a talent
discovery method it is helpful to know something about these tools:
who administers them, how they work and their value.

Prior to the 1920s career search methods did not exist; then
comparative tests to successful people in certain occupations were
devised. Early pioneers of interest testing were: T.L. Kelly, J.B. Wyman,
L.M. Terman and C.C. Miles. In the 1920s Edward K. Strong, Jr.
became the first to fully develop an interest inventory test backed
up by years of accumulated occupational data. Strong developed an
occupational interest test as an aid in the search for suitable occupations and careers for individuals. His objective was to match an
individual's test answers to the average answers of successful people
in eighty-nine select occupations. This comparative test further re-

duced the eighty-nine occupations to twenty-three basic interests and six general occupational themes.

David Campbell worked with Strong to further develop the Strong test, and later Campbell worked with Lenore W. Harmon to develop a Strong test for women. Kenneth Clark's Minnesota Vocational Interest Inventory and Frederic Kuder's Occupational Interest Survey among others added further refinements. Next came John L. Holland's Self Directed Search, Occupations Finder that expanded the number of occupations covered. Holland utilized Strong's themes and the Dept. of Labor D. O. T code system to develop a vocational aptitude and work temperament approach.

Test and search tools can be of help in career search, especially when administered by an experienced occupational guidance counselor. Tests are of value in locating interests and interest clusters that lead to occupations that may appeal to an individual.

Here is the problem: there are no tools that indicate what capabilities an individual may possess; therefore an individual cannot competently choose which of the 40,000 possible occupations would give him/her the best opportunity for health, happiness and success.

Each of us is the product of our genes, the environment and the experiences we have perceived through sight, smell, sound and touch. Most of what we see or hear is information that has been slanted to some degree to accomplish a purpose or to accommodate a story. Distortion and insufficient experience influence our answers on tests that identify our interests. A career consultant has no way of working with this distortion of interests.

Betty Edwards, who wrote Drawing on the Right Side of the Brain (St. Martins Press, New York, 1989), is a professor of art at California State University. In her lectures she says that most of us don't draw what we see in front of us but rather what we have already experienced and know. She solves the problem of the interference of childhood symbols in drawing by concentrating on negative space. As an example, when drawing a wood chair you turn it upside down so you cannot recognize what you are drawing and you find that you can make fairly good copies. The concentration is on the negative space. When drawing someone's portrait, forget the person's features. Draw in the dark areas and shadows and you would be surprised how well you can do.

How can we use a similar technique to bypass the slanted information that results in a misinterpretation of occupations?

Tests can tell us what you like or are interested in, not what you can do or do best.

Parents Need the Tests

A parent who does not take advantage of using professional consultants to help their child choose study courses and majors is taking a greater gamble than owning a home without fire insurance. A parent who commits to paying for their child's college education without using every tool they can to try to match the child's natural interests or capabilities to a field of study is making a mistake that can affect the child for life.

Tests should be conducted several times during a child's formative school years, so the counselor can see trends of interest taking place. With this interest information parents can attempt to expose their child to the interests and corresponding occupations (through the use of equipment, games, books, videos and visitations). The objective is to either substantiate or eliminate interests and to build a knowledge base of occupations. As the years pass a list of accumulated interests will start to build. With parent-guided exposure, this list can be invaluable in study and career search for the child. I am not saying that tests are perfect or even efficient but they are certainly helpful and better than nothing to work with.

Few school budgets commit to professional career counseling so the burden falls on teachers who do not have the experience or time to do professional counseling. I feel sorry for teachers who are required to give interest tests to students to be of help in student counseling. Sometimes when the teacher attempts to focus on one or more professions for the student, the student's irate parents confront the teacher because the parents may have other ideas for their child. Many parents are more interested in the child doing what the parent has in mind rather than what is good for the child. To attempt to steer a child into a career not amenable to that child's nature can have disastrous results.

Our occupation is all-important to us, for we spend most of our lives working, thinking, dreaming and worrying about work. It may effect where we live, our friends, whom we marry almost every aspect of our lives. If we choose the wrong occupation our lives are forever changed.

Every day millions of people try to remain in jobs they cannot possibly succeed at or stay in positions that are detrimental to their mental and/or physical health. We have been doing this so long that we cannot imagine it to be any different. Doctors tell us that stress caused by unnatural work functions is a substantial source of our health problems. People do not put up with ill-fitting clothing but they put up with ill-fitting occupations that can do much greater harm.

Some people who cannot find a use for their talents or meaningful work turn to anti-social or illegal activities to make a living. Once caught up in these acts it is hard for them to change course, at least without some method of identifying and supporting a direction that better suits their abilities.

According to the dictionary, "ability" means to be able to do something. To have an ability to do something very well, would be considered highly capable. To do it extremely well would be considered talent. Could each of us have some unknown talent we could do extremely well?

Should we be searching for occupations, careers or talent? Obviously talent would point to occupations that result in talented careers. It was therefore obvious that we should be looking for talent.

Talent continued to invade my thoughts. I would wake up at night thinking about it. What is talent? How can people know if they have a hidden talent? The stage was now set for me to find a needed method to identify an individual's talents.

One morning I awoke before dawn. In my mind was a picture of an octagon, each side labeled with something I had done in the past. It was as though a veil had been lifted. Suddenly, so many things started to make sense. The eight sides were:

1. My years of job changes in a wide variety of work.
2. My continuous preoccupation with interest tests.
3. The development of the "Select Profile System."
4. The development of the "Getting to Know You" exercise.
5. Taking on the responsibility of the Director of Vocational Guidance at Concordia University.
6. Setting up the Vocational Guidance Institute.
7. "Talent" constantly invading my sleep and writings.
8. My interest in doing something to help people find their talent. And, in the center, were two words: Talent Discovery.

I had a strange feeling my life had been pre-programmed to find a method to discover an individual's talent. That did not make sense to me. Why, with my simple background and inadequate education, would I be entrusted with the responsibility to discover a method of talent discovery? Considering all of the unusual circumstances I had been thrown into, it made me wonder if it was accidental.

Without knowing why, I am helpless to do anything but continue to pay attention to the direction I seemed compelled to follow. So, I continued to research and study what ever information was available about talent.

We Have Problems

It occurred to me that since I appear to have hidden talents education could not find, other people too could have hidden talents. The talent door may be open to everyone and to me is worth the search. However one question bothered me: "If talent is the valuable key to career search, why is it that people in the educational community are not desperately looking for a way to find individual talent?"

There are millions of capable, highly educated and intelligent people involved in education, career search and personnel management. Why aren't they searching for a method to discover individual talent? Could I be wrong?

No. Talent discovery has to be the valuable and valid process that we need to help individuals find their own high level of ability so they can adequately provide for their wants, needs and desires and solve their personal problems. Through a talent discovery method people would be able to find and utilize their natural born talents in an occupation, vocation or hobby. We need whatever special ability we are born with to solve our personal problems, acquire an identity and give our lives acceptable meaning and purpose. With these thoughts firmly established in my mind I continued to research talent and in the process I found discovering talents could have more than a personal value.

Value to Society

If more people are capable of accomplishing what precious few talented people have already done in electronics, space engineering, chemistry, genetics, etc. the effect on society and business would be outstanding. That being a fair assumption, our government and business leaders should have great interest in providing the effort and financial backing needed to find a method of talent discovery. It could be the best return on money they ever made.

We desperately need to find people with hidden talents who can solve society's problems. Imagine if we located thousands of people who could apply their talents to specific social issues. Serious problems could not persist in an onslaught of new ideas from a newly discovered wave of people talented in a specific field. One talent working alone is valuable; several working together more effective; thousands working together become a tidal wave that no problem could withstand. Talent discovery grows in importance.

Talented People

I have a copy of a drawing of a little boy exclaiming "If you don't like it you ain't going to be any good at it." Who can disagree? But what can we do about it if we don't know what we may be good at? We need a job, any job to support ourselves and a family. Jobs are hard to find in many areas. Some jobs are more difficult to do than others and some that appear to be good jobs at first are not. Less likable jobs sometimes pay better or offer more financial security. What are we to do?

On the other hand, who can argue that the services of people will be more valuable, efficient and productive when those people are working at activities they like and are talented at? Who can deny people talented in their work would be more interested and challenged? With less boredom, frustration, and stress, people have the ability to be more inventive, creative and capable at solving difficult problems.

These being acceptable factors, who would not support that talent discovery is one of the most important tasks that our educators, government and business leaders should pursue?

People such as Albert Einstein, Thomas Edison and Winston Churchill had learning disorders and may not have succeeded in centuries past. These men succeeded because they found a timely interest, and when exposed to a convenient environment found an area they were talented at.

All of us have known quiet, unnoticeable people who seemed

unlikely to succeed suddenly reappear on the scene and pass everyone else by. The one thing that these people have in common is they found a talent they possessed that society or business valued, a talent that gave them confidence and they took off.

So often when I interviewed people I sensed unknown ability. I could feel it and see it in their eyes: so much waiting to come out, so much to be done to make life interesting and fulfilling. Of the thousands of people I tested and interviewed all but a few left me with this feeling.

Talent seems to be lurking everywhere. It can suddenly appear at any place or time and in the most unlikely people. It is not limited by race, creed, education, family background or economics. We don't know how many different kinds talents there are. There must be thousands of specific activity combinations that could result in talent, we know we need them. A method to discover talent must be out there someplace, and no doubt it will be discovered one day.

In every known occupation there are probably many people with a specific talent but all slightly different. No two talents could be exactly alike as no two people are exactly alike. There are certainly useful talents we have not as yet heard of from which new occupations will be created.

Why do we know so little about talent? What is talent and where does it come from? There may be talent discovery research going on but after combing the libraries I could not find evidence of it. People seemed to accept talent as if to say: "Why take it apart? What purpose would that serve?"

Without established research I would have to form my own conclusions, and that is far from satisfactory. After all, who am I with so little knowledge and education to be delving into this highly professional area?

The complexity of all these questions and contradictions seemed at the time to be too much for me, therefore I attempted to set talent discovery aside and forget about it.

PART II

✦ ✦ ✦

THE SEARCH

*Somewhere under the stars God has a job for you
to do and nobody else can do it.*
HORACE BUSHNELL

7

Maximum Talent Capability
October 1987

Without assumptions we would not be able to
think at all. Assumptions are based on experience
and narrow down the range of possibilities of our
thinking. There is absolutely nothing wrong with
assumptions, which are most valuable.
Nevertheless it is useful to make ourselves aware of
the assumptions so that we can
choose to challenge them.
EDWARD DE BONO, *SERIOUS CREATIVITY*

When I was still active in business, our sales representative in the Middle East requested that I visit Egypt to meet government officials who were in charge of Egypt's fertilizer plants. The Egyptian officials had run substantial tests on our waste enzymes used to control corrosion and bacteria in their fertilizer plant cooling systems, a difficult and expensive problem. They were ready to commit a substantial yearly contract to us for our enzymes but insisted they meet the president or owner of the company before they presented their letters of credit in advance of shipment. As owner and president I was required to go. My wife, Donna and I decided to include the trip to Egypt in our vacation by taking a cruise on the Nile River.

As the *HS. Hotp* moved quietly up the ancient river we could see how the desert closes in on the narrow band of farm land between the mountains of sand and the river. At times the high sand looked like a menacing snow avalanche waiting to reclaim its land down to the river.

Sitting up on the deck late at night by myself, watching the moon weave its light into the water of the Nile was eerie and strange. There seemed to be a presence that engulfed me, a feeling as though the ancients were still every where and I had somehow been a part of them thousands of years ago.

Suddenly the word talent crossed my mind. Then two questions: Why should talent be limited to a special few? Why should one person have talent ability more than another? Then a strange thought invaded my mind. It said, "Everything lapses. Time and years mean nothing. Face the truth of what you believe, no matter how strange it may seem at this fleeting moment in time."

What a strange occurrence and usage of words. What did "fleeting moment" and "time" refer to? Is it possible the statement referred to a thought that had recently crossed my mind. "Not just some, but all people may have a hidden talent capability."

That statement was just too unbelievable to admit, and still as I watched the moon's shadow on the distant sand dunes I somehow knew it had to be true.

Everyone has a maximum talent capability in some unknown area, something they can do better than anything else.

There it is. I said it, and I know why I have denied the concept for so long. The implications are difficult to accept. Everyone having unknown talent capability would shake the foundations of education and society. I had instinctively known all people may have a maximum talent and now I am compelled to accept it. But, if all people have a talent capability, how can it be located, identified or proven? Would it help to take a closer look at an individual?

Human Physical Activity

All people are normally born with two legs, two arms, two hands, two eyes, one nose and a three-pound brain. Even brains that weigh a little more or a little less than three pounds have the same genetic structure and functional ability.

It is not normal to be born with seven fingers on each hand or an eye in the back of the head. That would be a utility advantage that some people would have over others. If God gave each of us equality in our physical makeup; why should it be different when it comes to talent? Why should only certain people have a talent capability?

Talent may be like an arm or a leg: everyone has one. All of us humans have the same necessary and complete DNA genetic building blocks; we could not come into being if we did not. If some one has genes that make efficient ability available; then all of us must have those genes. Isn't it therefore possible that we all have a maximum talent in some unknown area? This then could be a natural human trait, it is logical and makes sense.

However, during my research I did not find scientific data to support the fact that everyone has talent; and being logical or making sense does not prove the theory. Some people may find this concept difficult to accept and some may reject it for personal reasons. Other people will be extremely critical and demand substantiation; as yet there is none, we know so little of our abilities.

The search for an individual's "maximum talent capability" is now, by necessity, the focus of this search. When looking for answers, most discoveries start from ideas and assumptions. Let's see how far I can get in the search for proof.

Maximum talent capability is a strange combination of words. I wonder how my mind put them together. I can see myself walking up to someone at a cocktail party and asking: "What is your maximum talent capability?"

"My what?"

"Your maximum talent capability?"

"You must be drinking some very potent stuff, You'd better watch it."

"No. I'm serious. Of all the things in this world, what can you do better than anything else?"

"How do I know? I haven't done everything!"

He would be right. Who could possibly have done every different task there is to do in all occupations? How could he know what he could do best? How could he be exposed to all occupations? There is much work to be done with "maximum talent capability," I would imagine in time others may shorten it to "maxtalability."

Uneducated People may Have Talent

It occurred to me that if all people have hidden talent capability, the uneducated may be included. And why not? Perhaps education's inability to search out individual talent is why many people remain uneducated. Once the uneducated know their talents, it could raise their interest and confidence. Now they too could be productive and make greater contributions to society. Talent may give them the identity and self esteem they have desperately been longing for. Many of these people may with discovered talents want to learn with a vengeance.

One of my pre-edit readers asked me. "You mean that we could take a dropout off the street, someone with apparently low intellect and minimum learning ability, like Eliza's 'The Rain in Spain' diction performance in *My Fair Lady*, and transform that person into a highly talented individual?"

"Yes, it appears that may be possible."

"Boy, you are a dreamer."

"Perhaps, but I have no doubt it will be accomplished in the future. Why not start now, when we need it so badly?"

Talent does not often surface in school. Class reunions reveal people who are outstanding successes, in spite of the fact that while they were in school they were poor students and seemed the least likely to succeed. How do we account for this?

The Egyptian, Japanese and Chinese languages utilize hieroglyphic symbols instead of an alphabet. Is it possible if our language was hieroglyphic some of our literate people would be illiterate and some illiterates literate? Interpreting a picture (hieroglyphic) requires imagination; words require interpretation. Do illiterate people have a better imagination? We cannot overlook the possibility. I have seen illiterates show surprising ingenuity and capability. Maybe for some people our form of written communication encourages illiteracy.

Imagine it was possible to discover individual talent; we could change our current education system so individuals were educated according to their talents. Accordingly, the talents of teachers would be known, and the groups of students with similar talents would be instructed by teachers who shared the same talents. Interested and talented students being taught by talented teachers, that would be quite a change. Talents need to be discovered, released, and nurtured. Everyone should have the opportunity to achieve what is believed to be talent status. Talent exists in all of us; we only need to find a method of discovering it.

What is Talent?

Maxtalability arises when an individual's talents are combined with a compatible occupation. It is possible we will find several talent capabilities in each individual. How do we find these talents? Would a trial and error method work (similar to the football team observation method)?

Consider the following: a person who cannot tolerate the sight of blood would not make a good doctor, a person who is able to work with blood is on the first step towards becoming a doctor, a person who can endure the sight of blood but is not skillful with his or her hands would not make a good surgeon, a person who cannot tolerate heights would not do well as a bridge mechanic, a person who enjoys heights is on the first step to becoming a bridge mechanic, etc. There are literally hundreds of activities involved in only these two fields: medicine and bridge maintenance. Each of the activities will either confirm or deny an individual's suitability in these occupations. The higher the capability in all of the necessary activities of a profession, the more the person's talent approaches maximum capability. What is it within us that makes this qualification or distinction? This is a lot to think about.

Back to Egypt

I never did meet with the Egyptian officials on this trip. However for my purpose it was a most worthwhile and mystical trip; one that left a strong and enduring impression on me. The ancients on the Nile may have given me the benefit of their wisdom and made me face the truth of what I had come to believe. Every individual has a maximum talent capability in some area; and talent seems to be a combination of physical and mental abilities.

Since thought originates in the brain, I decided that upon my return from Egypt I would expand my library to include any research that was available on the human brain and mind. Although occasionally interesting reading, it was mostly technical and dull. From what I was able to interpret, most psychologists considered the mind the activity area of the brain (I shall use that interpretation as we proceed). There appeared to be little work done in the area of thought origination in regard to talent.

I shifted my study back to talent. To find maximum talent capability, we must know as much about talent as possible. As a society, we appear to have taken talent for granted. To my knowledge, no research had been done to find out what talent is. Before I could determine where talent originated or how it functioned I needed to know what it was. I wondered if it was possible to take talent apart and examine it? Without previous research, how could that possibly be done?

When we returned to Milwaukee, pressing business matters temporarily left me little time to think about talent.

8

Work can be Hazardous
to Your Health

*Someday the principles of vocational guidance will
be employed as well as those of vocational selection.
Then there will be concern for fitting not only men
into jobs but jobs into men.*
EDWARD K. STRONG JR.,
VOCATIONAL INTERESTS OF MEN AND WOMEN

Research has shown that people who have or are subject to
negative emotions or depression are substantially more sus-
ceptible to disease, many lack the will to live. Our bodies
are a mirror of our emotions; negative emotions can weaken our
immune system, perhaps by limiting the chemicals needed to remain strong and healthy. Human emotions are subject to depression, guilt, fear, suppressed anger, being unloved or lack of confidence or lack of faith.

What percentage of your adult life do you spend at work, going
to and from work, working at home, talking about work, thinking
about work, and dreaming about work? I have read that it is about
seventy percent! If this large part of your life is not positive and
challenging, how will you be affected?

There seems to be a definite connection between your work environment and your health and how long you will live. Evidence

shows that people who feel they serve a purpose through meaningful interests remain active and live longer, healthier lives.

Researchers at U.C.L.A. found that people with a history of stress in the workplace have more than five times the risk of developing colon and rectal cancer than those who enjoy their work. Workers in a working environment that is not compatible with their nature are more prone to accidents? Could work or an occupation that is negative to an individual's natural attributes shorten lives as much as a year, five years, ten years . . . twenty-five? Researchers are starting to believe so. Your work may control how well and how long you live.

Negative or Raw Talent

In the search for an individual's talent and in my attempts to take talent apart, I could not help but recognize a substantial difference between positive and negative talent. An individual can have both positive and negative talents, sometimes only the negative may surface. We all know people who seem happy, relaxed and content with their lives. Could people be using some of their positive talent abilities? Could people who are fraught with anxiety and fear brought on by stress be using negative talent abilities? Will their frustration ultimately destroy their health? Many successful people who are driven by ambition find negative talent to exploit as an outlet for their motivation.

I refer to some negative talents as "raw" because in time they tend to wear a person emotionally raw, like a blister on a heel. I have witnessed many successful individuals who are in occupations that require activities that grate against their personalities, depreciate their ethics, and ruin their health and marriages.

People can accidentally stumble on an activity that is not good for their well-being; and if it is the only useful activity they know, it is natural to use it; but can they live with it? So often famous people say: "Something is missing from my life." People in a highly-visible occupation, such as entertainment, may require that they use some of their negative talents, making their lives difficult and unhappy.

Some people in high-level jobs know when stress is affecting their well-being and give it all up for a quieter existence. Were their minds and bodies telling them they were in the wrong occupation, and therefore placing themselves in harm's way? There are a great number of retired people who could trace physical defects in retirement to an area of their working lives, it is tragic; and perhaps through talent discovery it can be preventable. Could each individual have a different and measurable stress tolerance for each one of the vast number of occupations or at least certain activities involved in occupations?

Negative talent does not only affect the individual. Others who are dependent or responsive to them, especially their families, are affected as well. People involved in negative talent often find their marriages fall victim as emotional problems develop. I found that the percentage of highly successful people who remained married to the spouse they had before their success is quite small.

A negative talent can become addictive as it provides for wants, needs and desires. Negative-talented people may try to convince themselves they are happy with what they have accumulated rather than what they have become. Some are inwardly scared and would rather "chuck it all" if they could. It is not uncommon for people to become brilliant in a career that is not compatible with their well-being. Negative talent creates excessive external identity at the sacrifice of internal well being and it is difficult to ignore public applause.

Take an example of four entertainers. Marilyn Monroe died at the age of thirty-six and Elvis Presley at age forty-two; both had difficult personal lives. Compare them with George Burns, still going strong at ninety-nine, and Bob Hope, still active at ninety-two. Are these examples of people using negative and positive talents?

Negative work creates an environment that is the source of ulcers, heart problems, cancer, and even self destruction; as it grinds against an individual's mental, physical and emotional health. People may self destruct by unconsciously withholding chemicals from their immune system.

Dr. Ichiro Kawachi, assistant professor of health and social behavior at the Harvard School of Public Health and his team, found that people scoring high on an anxiety scale were four and one half times more likely to die of a heart attack. So-called hot reactors to stress have increased the risk of cardiovascular disease and the risk increases with age.

Negative talent can cause anxiety that ultimately results in friction. The suicide and attempted suicide rate among successful and highly-talented people suggests that talent may be a two-sided coin: positive in material benefits but negative to health and longevity.

Then again negative talent should be closely examined. It may consist of a combination of both negative and positive. Its positive or negative nature may depend upon how or where the activity is utilized. Certain activities in a talent may not be healthy for a fulltime occupation but may loose the negative effect when used in part-time work, hobbies or recreation. No talent should be ignored; all talents should be analyzed for positive use.

Do You Love Your Job?

Quite often I have been puzzled by how people describe or react to their jobs when I ask strangers how they feel about their work. One minute they say they love their jobs and the next they are describing how bad it can be. What does a person mean when they say they love their job? Many say they love their work; however, when asked specific questions, it becomes obvious that "love" may be more of a cliché than the right word to describe their feelings about their jobs.

The following are some of the questions I had asked individuals who appeared to be interested and not offended by the conversation:

+ What would you delete from your job to make it more enjoyable?
+ What would you want to do more of in your job to make it more enjoyable?
+ What would you want to do less of in your job to make it more enjoyable?
+ Have you developed or do you have any ideas as to how your job could be made better?
+ Is your job as challenging as you would like, is it fulfilling?
+ Is there something about your job you would want to write a book about?
+ Is there something you have thought of that would contribute to or move your profession forward?
+ What could you create about your job that would benefit humanity?
+ Do you want to do this job the rest of your life?
+ How can you use the knowledge of your work in retirement?
+ Would you be interested in doing so?
+ Would you do it? If no or hesitant, why not?
+ After you leave this world, what mark would you have left behind or what would you say you contributed to this world through your job?
+ Do you love your job or do you love what it provides you; both personally and in material things?

I had to be very careful in selecting and asking these questions because they can be very provoking. The reaction and direction of the conversation would tell me how far I could go.

What many people imply is their jobs, rather than their nonworking hours provide them more of what they need or prefer; their jobs are more satisfying than their leisure time. Some people need satisfying jobs because work compliments their leisure time. Your love life, family, friends and health can be great but if the most time-consuming area of your life, your job, is not satisfying it can discolor all other areas of your life.

Unless your work remains interesting and challenging, is physically and emotionally healthful, is rewarding and fulfilling, and you are able to leave a mark behind saying "you were here," you may never know true happiness from what you spent the majority of your life doing.

You may say in response to that: "Ah, but that is work perfection, an impossibility." Is it? Once I thought such a perfect work opportunity did not exist for us; now I'm not so sure.

Try this test to see if your work provides all of these things and to what degree. Taking this test may give you an idea as to what the benefits of your own maximum talent capability could be for you.

(There can be other attributes of work that are temporarily or permanently important to different people, such as people, places and things; but it is difficult to remove just one of the following attributes from a meaningful life's work.)

Be honest as you decide which of the words at the top of the chart best answer the following questions about your work.

Poor	Fair	Acceptable	Good	Excellent	Nearly Perfect

Are you talented at your job?
Is it interesting?
Is it challenging?
Is it physically and emotionally healthful?
Is every aspect of it completely honest and ethical?
Is the income rewarding?
Is it fulfilling?
Is it useful in retirement?
Will your work leave a positive mark on humanity?

How does your job or profession measure up against these questions? An individual's maximum talent capability if found could substantially satisfy these questions. I don't mean to imply that a maxtalability would be perfect because things involving humans never are. The object is to find an occupation or occupations that best applies an individual to his work in the most efficient and therefore near perfect application.

Maximum talent capability if and when found, developed and pursued could be like releasing an emergency brake that you have been driving with "on" all of your life. Your life may be dramatically more wonderful than it is; it only remains for you to have the opportunity to find your maxtalability.

Positive Talent

Each of us may be born with talents we have not discovered, so we work at jobs and professions not ideally suited to our physical and mental makeup. There can be no question that using positive talent is easier to live with than work that uses negative talent. When utilizing their positive talents people will find it easier to gain recognition and salary increases, and to obtain and retain promotions.

People working at jobs that they love, doing things that are good for their mental and physical health seldom get into trouble. Those who are involved in a profession that is not compatible with their mental and physical health develop problems. Negative talent can produce or force negative actions; positive talent results in positive results.

Social problems from juvenile delinquency, drugs, divorce and crime can be attributed to the lack of a positive identity or self esteem. Self esteem and positive identity can be found in the discovery of an individual's positive talent. Psychoanalyst Eric Erickson coined the phrase "identity crisis." Negative raw talent will not solve the identity crisis; positive talent can.

Those who are out of work or who have given up trying for a decent job may have talents that they do not know; positive talents that could elevate them out of their circumstances. The tragedy is that without knowing their talents people must take jobs negative to them because that is all there is. They have no alternative if they are to survive; and in time, their hopes and dreams are stifled.

I don't believe anyone alive today has the remotest idea of how valuable discovering his/her maxtalability could be to the quality of his/her life. Finding positive talent could be a lifesaver to many people; our work and our health are closely responsible to each other. In selecting among several maximum talent capabilities it may be difficult to know negative effect without experiencing the negative talent over a period of time. Some method of qualification is needed to interpret positive and negative effect. Is there a way of making a pre-distinction?

What have we learned so far? We have made the distinction between talent which may be negative and harmful and talent that is positive and beneficial. We have identified the attributes of maximum talent capability. We still need a method to identify the difference between negative and positive talent; and we still do not know what talent is or do we know how to find an individual's maximum talent.

Finding talents that are healthful and could lengthen the lives of people is a heavy responsibility. I want to help find the method if I can but am I the one to do it? I wonder what I'm getting myself into. I am not educated or qualified to do such technical study and reasoning without the support of established research.

I fear my theories will only result in disputes from professionals who feel I am trespassing on their territory. As a sensitive person maybe I should stay away from this pursuit and let more qualified professionals continue with the research. But who? Does anyone else believe all people may have unknown talents? Does anyone believe a method may exist to discover talents? Does anyone care enough to do something about it? Reluctantly I move forward. I cannot keep the pressing need for discovering talent from invading my mind even though I have little chance of finding it?

9

Talents and Human Activity

*If we are concerned with the shortage of talent in
our society, we must inevitably give attention to
those who have never explored their talents fully,
to all those who level off short of their full ceiling.
If we ever learn how to salvage any respectable
fraction of these, we will have unlocked a great
storehouse of talent.*

JOHN W. GARDNER, *EXCELLENCE*

According to dictionaries talent is: "a gift, endowment or facility of a superior kind, mental power, artistic aptitude, less than genius, special or outstanding ability." If that is what talent is, what causes it? Where does it come from? What is its makeup? How does it operate? How can we find talent if we do not know these factors?

I said to myself, "How am I going to make something out of this span of dictionary words? It tells me nothing. Science has not researched talent to give us clues to its make up. Why? How can they ignore such an important human faculty? I need help."

"Don't panic."

"I'm not! . . . wha . . . " Looking around I see no one. "Who and where the heck are you?"

"I'm Henry."

"Who is Henry and what are you doing invading my thoughts?"

"I'm your helper and you asked for help."

I looked around again. There was no one there. "You're invisible, huh?"

"Yup."

"How come you didn't come around before."

"Not allowed to. You got to ask."

"Hmph, funny name. Henry the helper?"

"So?"

"You can help?"

"Try me."

"This is crazy. Well all right, I'll go along. How are we going to find talent with those dictionary words?"

"Let's assume you have talent at writing."

"I doubt it; but go on."

"What are you doing when you're writing?"

"I'm thinking, creating and developing ideas, and typing them into the computer."

"What are those actions?"

"Hm. Let's see. Well I guess those are work or job tasks."

"Good, now let's eliminate work tasks. Job tasks and work tasks appear to be the same thing. What is a job task?"

"It's an activity or action a person performs."

"What does the dictionary say about activity and action?"

I took out my notes. "Activity, state or quality of being active; active faculty; active force; nimbleness; to do. Action, the state or manner of acting or being active; an act or thing done; the performance of a function; a deed; behavior; physical movement; function; flex action, involuntary motor reaction to a sensory impulse. Okay, Henry, what are we going to do with that?"

"I'm thinking. Not many words to help us know what talent is. We will have to make do."

"While you're thinking," I said, "let's see what I can put together. An occupation is made up of job tasks made up of actions or activity, and they must be initiated by some area of the brain. Now what?"

"Keep going, you're doing fine."

"Aren't you going to help?" I asked.

"Not supposed to do your work for you. What is the problem with that statement?"

"Actions and activity need to be clarified," I stated. "Let's see, an activity could have actions but it does not seem right for actions to have activities. Action is a physical movement and an activity is made up of a number of actions. An activity is like a simple story. An action has no story; it is just a movement. A job task could consist of several activity stories."

"Very good," coached Henry, "but there are lots of activities. Are we interested in all of them?"

"There are many references to activity: chemical, economic, mechanical, and activities of nature. Oh, I see what you mean. We are interested only in physical and mental activity, in other words human activity. Hey, that's not bad."

"Good boy, that ought to help. See ya."

"Hey, where are you going?"

"I'm done for the night." Blip.

"Hey!" I protested. No answer. "He's gone. Wonder where he came from? I must have been talking to myself."

At the library I looked up human activity. Nothing. There were fifteen hundred references on activity but nothing on activity-human. What do I do now?

Let's analyze what we now know. I have occupations made up of job tasks, job tasks made up of human activities, and human activities made up of actions that are mentally initiated from some area of the brain and physically performed. That is how it must work, but who else knows or cares about this? No one that I could find, so hesitantly and unsure I continue.

Talent is comprised of job tasks, human activities and actions, but how do those things result in talent?

"Help! Henry?" No answer. I must have been daydreaming about Henry.

I continued to research the human brain and mind, specifically looking for something on their workings and capabilities. The brain is a series of compartments, each responsible for a certain function. One might believe that there is a capability compartment, except for one factor, when we disturb one compartment we find that all neurons are interconnected in a neuron network. The number of neurons in the cortex of the brain alone is estimated at ten thousand million, that is quite a figure and the connectivity of that many neurons is endless. There is not much hope at this stage in brain research of placing our finger on a single source of capability or talent; it could run throughout the brain and somehow through the entire body.

Reading late at night is hard on the eyes, especially wading through a maze of bland brain research. Finally I could only conclude that if society had to depend on brain science for a discovery of talent our generation would not be alive for the answer. We can only go back to job tasks and activity to find another opening to continue.

It appears talent consists of job tasks that involve activities and actions. If this premise is to hold up, I needed to find what elevates this combination of activities and actions to talent status. In such a vast area of the unknown, where and what could that possibly be?

10

Human Activity and Efficiency
August 1990

*Fate gives every single one of us the most
astonishing uniqueness. Each person is a complex
mesh of finely woven styles, viewpoints, abilities,
tastes, and gifts. There's no one in the world that
can do what you can do, who can think and see the
way you do, who can create what you can create.*
BARBARA SHER,
I COULD DO ANYTHING IF I ONLY KNEW WHAT IT WAS

Each activity is a story that has a beginning and an end. It
leaves an impression of something accomplished. Actions are
the motions required to carry out and complete an activity.
Let's take a closer look at activity to see if there is anything there
that will open a door for us. An activity must be of interest, a constant or growing challenge, or it becomes boring. Some workers can
turn their mind off to a repetitive and/or boring job activity and
they become robotic. The brain knows if it wants to continue doing
an activity over and over again and can therefore pass judgment on
a repetitive activity. Interesting, but still this does not tell me what
lifts certain occupations (consisting of job tasks, activities and the
required actions) to talent status.

Researching talent at the library, I fail to discover a lead. I seem
to be at a dead end.

Jackson Hole, Wyoming

Donna wanted to see Yellowstone National Park. I had seen it in 1936 when I was fourteen years old and I had always wanted to visit Jackson Hole, just south of Yellowstone. We flew to Salt Lake City in August 1990, rented a car and drove to Jackson Hole.

It was as I visualized it: a high, remote valley surrounded by mountains, forest wilderness, clear cold lakes, beautiful rivers and roaring river canyons leading out of the valley. Since there is not a railroad in Jackson Hole, the valley seemed even more remote and virginal.

I fell in with love with Jackson Hole and from its historic background I was inspired to write a turn-of-the-century novel about a young woman with a special mental ability (no doubt brought on by all of my reading about the brain). Usually a story like this comes on when I have a problem to solve. The story poured forth with great ease and hangs together so well I may call it The Gros Ventre Story. I have to polish and finish it someday.

What took my mind back to talent was an incident that took place at the Spring Creek Resort located on top of the East Gros Ventre Butte in Jackson Hole. Donna and I were having a cocktail on the timbered terrace of the Resort restaurant before dinner. We were enchanted by the change in colors as the sun slowly set behind the Tetons.

I was sitting quietly, appreciating the view, when the word talent penetrated my mind. So often new ideas or solutions come to me at quiet times in remote places, when I am surrounded by wilderness and scenes of great beauty. Now, here on this high butte, my brain decides to invade my thoughts about talent again. So go ahead, brain, louse up my reverie. Let's see what you have.

Everyone is constantly active. Everyone has activity capability, it is built in, automatic. We can't live without it, activity is necessary for survival. Everyone is interested in or has a preference for different activities. We might say each individual has their own activity preference personality.

We can describe activity as talented when the activity performance is conducted at a high level of efficiency. Efficiency? Hmm, very interesting. Activity? . . . Efficiency?

So what is talent other than a highly efficient activity in some specific area? Let's say that again. Talent is a highly efficient activity or a combination of highly efficient activities working together in some particular area. Further more talent could not be a scattering of unrelated activities; That was it. We all have talent when we perform a group of required activities at a high level of efficiency. I also think the required activities would have to compliment each other in some way. That may be what lifts an activity to talent status. Who can refute that we all have a higher level of efficient activity capability in a certain areas in which we are more capable at than others we might do? A combination of efficient activities working efficiently together results in a talent or more specifically a maximum talent capability. I jerked up, almost spilling my drink. "Wow," I formed with my mouth.

Donna was talking to a lady seated next to her. She turned to me. "Something the matter?" she asked with concern.

"I've been looking for an answer for so long and suddenly a simple and obvious answer came to me," I answered.

She smiled. "Oh, well I'm glad," she said vaguely, not quite sure what I was talking about. Donna respects my work and knows that I take my writing seriously; but as a novice writer I sometimes get carried away discussing my work with friends and guests. Donna turned back to her conversation with the woman next to her and I went back to thinking about talent.

Maximum talent capability is an efficient combination of skillful activities that would have to be sponsored by genes! "Genes?" I said out loud. Now where did that come from? Donna gave me a frown for that outburst. There were other people on the porch but they were busy talking and paid no attention to me. I put my hand over my mouth. No more outbursts like that.

In just a few minutes two words related to activity surfaced: efficiency and genes. Maximum talent capability is a combination of efficient human activities performed by actions that could be sponsored by efficient genes. Efficient genes? I have to research that. Genes create and control us, so genes must be the source of actions that make up activity. There it was and it made sense. Where does this stuff come from? It does leave a question though: Are efficient genes necessary to create efficient activities?

After dinner we returned to our rustic room. Someone had lit the fireplace. Donna, an early riser, kissed me goodnight and went to bed. I had more thinking to do; so I put on a warm jacket, opened the sliding glass door and sat on our private balcony facing the fantastic view of the Tetons. The valley was in all shades of blue and purple with the Snake River far below reflecting a silver ribbon of light, and the glacier high in the saddle of the Grande Teton glowing with absorbed light.

So, the question to consider was, how does activity efficiency relate to talent? Everyone may not have what the public recognizes as talent, but everyone has one or more capabilities in which they could be more efficient at than any others they have been involved with. As an example, in school by trial and error and competition we can recognize the sport or a particular position in a sport a student can do best. This same recognition method cannot be done with 40,000 occupations. Let's analyze occupational work:

  ✦ Each occupation is performed through a number of job tasks
  ✦ Each job task is performed by a number of activities.
  ✦ Each activity is performed by a number of physical actions.

Some activities may be repeated in many job tasks but even then there must be thousands of different human activities. There is no way to submit an individual to the thousands of activities many of which they may not even be aware or have knowledge of. This precludes using trial and error or competition to find which activities an individual is most efficient at. There has to be another way.

How many different activities are there and what does the whole panorama of human activities look like? Every one of the estimated 40,000 occupations must consist of a human doing certain job tasks, each task requiring a different combination of mental and physical activities. Each occupation may have its own job tasks profile, each job task its own activity profile and each activity its own action profile. Each of these profiles may be subject to the environment where they are performed.

This clarifies the activity principles we have to work with but it does not answer what controls and effects or enhances efficiency.

Maxtalability is a combination of required and closely related highly efficient activities, supported by actions that are modified by some specific action or energy. How can efficient genes and some kind of energy modify these activities to talent status?

Thought Patterns

It occurred to me there must be more to activity. The brain obviously initiates human activity. Mind and body have to work together or no activity occurs. The mind can think of something without requiring physical action because thinking by itself would appear to be an activity. The mind may have to develop a thought pattern; like a blueprint of an activity it wants the physical parts of the body to perform. Thought patterns may not be the source and the sponsors of activity but do they effect efficiency? Science claims we use little of the brain's thought capacity (I read that humans use less than five percent of their brain). The brain may be capable of endless thoughts through its neuron network. A mental activity uses the neuron pathways of the mind to develop thought patterns; which is far more complicated than physical activity.

Inspiration

If thought patterns originate in the neurons of the brain, what instigates a thought pattern? Some researchers think it has something to do with inspiration. The dictionary states that inspiration is something "conveyed to the mind under extraordinary influence," and "influence emanating from any object giving rise to new and elevated thoughts and emotions." If inspiration gives rise to thought patterns, what gives rise to inspiration? Imagination? If so what gives rise to imagination? That is really deep. Let's get back to inspiration and see if something of help is there.

Where does inspiration start? Is it genetic? Are there inspiration genes? Genes can create a finger but do they create inspiration? A finger is a physical thing; inspiration has no material substance and may be temporary.

When an individual comes close to one of their efficient talent activities inspiration may somehow indicate to the individual he/she is near to a talent area and because of it inspiration sparks an interest. Is this intuition? Everyone has maximum talent capabilities so if it is intuition, why doesn't intuition bring talent to the surface?

Little is known about inspiration and intuition. They are less than smoke that has no substance; but at least we can temporarily see smoke. This seems far afield from our problems of efficiency and synergism, but in the future someone may find inspiration and intuition as they relate to talent worth researching.

There are two schools of thought about where talent comes from. One holds that talent is genetic and inherited and the other that it is environmentally developed and learned. Both schools may be right. Physical activity could be genetically limited because it is of the body or bodily anchored, mental activity is not so anchored and therefore, may not be genetically limited.

A thought pattern is invisible but it is an activity no less; though more complex and difficult to understand. I found there is research being started on thought patterns but nothing I could use presently. For now it was enough to know where thought patterns originated.

Human Activities-Synergistic

It became very cool out on the balcony so I started to get up to go in by the fireplace when my brain flung this at me: There is present within each individual certain human activities or traits in which they can excel in synergistic combination and application that makes every common man uncommon.

That's profound and strange. Where did synergistic come from? First efficiency, then genes, and now synergistic. Could all of these be involved in talent somehow?

In chemistry, when certain inactive chemicals are combined, a release of energy can occur, creating a new compound. Independently, the inactive chemicals would not react or release any energy.

Several human activities brought together and applied to specific occupations or job tasks may be subject to the same synergistic principle; but how does synergism modify an efficient group of activities?

Enough for the night. That's a lot to digest and write down. My mind was ablaze. What a great night. These were wondrous breakthroughs that gave me much to think about. I prayed that they would fall into place in the talent picture. My eyes focused on the Grand Tetons in the distance and the night sky above, full of diamond stars. I was cold. How long had I been sitting out there? My watch said several hours. Inside sitting by the warm mesquite fire, I recorded these new thoughts and ideas.

Cataloguing Human Activities

While flying back to Milwaukee, I thought off and on about human activity. Once we landed, I headed for the library at the University of Wisconsin/Milwaukee to find out how many human activities there are and how they are catalogued.

I punched activity into the computer and scanned through hundreds of entries. Nothing referred to the cataloguing, coding or describing of human activities. I had hoped that someone would have already catalogued and coded all human activities. Occupation catalogues and codes won't help me; I needed one that was based on human activities.

It seemed as if no one ever questioned human activity before; and all of us are involved with activities everyday. I found information about thought patterns but nothing organized or related to human activities. I found the same results at the Milwaukee public library . . . nothing on human activity. I could not believe it. There was also nothing about synergism or genes as they related to human activity.

One listing I found that might be helpful in breaking down human activities was in the *Dictionary of Occupational Titles* set up by the U.S. Department of Labor. It listed the following worker functions that may be general rather than specific activities:

DATA
    ANALYZING
    SYNTHESIZING
    COORDINATING-INNOVATING
    COMPILING-COMPUTING
    COPYING
    COMPARING

PEOPLE
    MENTORING
    NEGOTIATING
    INSTRUCTING
    SUPERVISING
    DIVERTING-PERSUADING
    SPEAKING-SIGNALING
    SERVING-TAKING INSTRUCTIONS-HELPING

THINGS
   SETTING UP
   PRECISION WORKING
   OPERATING-CONTROLLING
   DRIVING-OPERATING
   MANIPULATING
   TENDING
   FEEDING-OFFBEARING-HANDLING

These few functions, as an example, could be main headings of a job task and human activity coding system. Let's try the function of "analyzing." I wonder how deep analyzing might sub-divide a job task to distinct human activities?

The Wall Street Journal has listed a hundred different industry groups. To find the usage of "analyzing" I will multiply "analyzing" by one hundred different industry groups (analyzing would be subject to different products and services in each of these industry groups).

In each of the hundred industry groups there are conceivably thousands of companies who analyze their own products and services differently. Furthermore, each department in each of these companies analyzes for different purposes according to that department's requirement. In essence, "analyzing" can be divided and subdivided many times. It is an activity that takes on a different character according to what is being analyzed. Certain analyzing activities may be common to many companies and others quite rare.

As I penetrated deeper, the function of analyzing takes on a distinct personality when it is subjected to different environments and people. When we subdivide things people work with, we have further expanded the number of activity divisions taking place.

Let's take a diverting-persuading function as an example. Persuading is a method of selling. Selling differs by the type of product and service being sold. Selling transportation vehicles can be broken down into: airplanes, trains, buses, light trucks, heavy trucks, autos, motorcycles and bicycles. One person is probably more successful at selling one vehicle over another. In reality, these are all different activities: selling different vehicles to different people in different places. This being true, there should be one or more products or services a particular salesperson is more talented at selling than any other product or service. A method or way to find the maximum talent for that specific individual is what we are looking for. To arrive at a true measure of the activity efficiency of an individual by exposure to that activity, we may have to reduce an activity to where it is no longer subject to change by environment or people. This tells me how very complicated human activities can become. Let's look for another way.

Another catalogue approach may be through breaking down the over 40,000 occupations into their required job tasks and then breaking the job tasks down to activities. To work with the activities they should be coded and entered onto a computer. (How this is done will be up to the professionals who design, catalogue and code the job tasks.)

None of this conjecture tells us how many distinct human activities exist. Why is human activity such an unknown subject? Could I be wrong? No way. Talent is highly efficient human activity. How else could you describe or measure the different activities people do daily? Very puzzling!

For a while my mind was blank and I made no headway. I had made such progress in uncovering efficiency, genes and synergism; but how can I prove they affect talent? Why hasn't anyone catalogued job tasks and human activities? Doesn't anyone care about how humans do things? What could be more important? It will be difficult enough to solve the talent problem; now a way must be found to catalogue the job tasks and human activities of 40,000 occupations. It will take a large staff, be expensive and time consuming. How can I possibly do this? Will this obstacle prevent the discovery and development of a Maxtalability method?

I needed to rest my mind for a while, so I decided to finish the Gros Ventre story. Alas, my mind wanted to dwell on a new novel that also takes place in Jackson Hole. I named the story "McClellan Valley."

The story is about a shy, young college student who is about to drop out of college for lack of funds and college direction. He has a rare skin condition that on contact with any other person's skin within hours erupts the surface of his skin with bloody lacerations, similar to the effect of a flash fire.

Each time it happens the condition worsens. He has a dream of a normal life; for him almost impossible considering his skin condition. He is led to believe (by a mysterious and aging professor) he has a talent that will allow him to accomplish anything, including his dream of a valley and a girl who may never touch him. In addition to his skin problem, there is a requirement that is going to be hard for this shy young man to do. From this required effort a synergistic and mystical aura starts to develop.

This synergistic aura or field of energy from the story stuck in my mind demanding attention; but I could not make sense of it at the time. At the same time the question of who would care about cataloguing human activities continued to nag me.

Robots

Upon retiring one night I posed a question to my subconscious to work on while I was sleeping: "Who would care about cataloguing human activities and actions?" At 3:00 a.m. I woke up with a start. "Robotics?" People working with robotics would care about human movements. They study human movements to develop a robot to do human work. Robots are designed to simulate and replace humans.

So I investigate robotics. Yes, people in this field have studied certain human physical actions and thought patterns but I still do not find a catalogue or listing of human activities.

Robotics is more concerned with human actions than with human activity.

One observation that came out of robotics was a look towards the future, when robots will displace blue collar workers until there are very few labor jobs left. Especially with the combination of increased automation and employee-sponsored law suits, most manual or labor intensive work may disappear. There may be an attempt to make industry focus more on human labor requirements but it will likely not succeed as it is a contradiction to progress and economics.

Today when a new plant is built, it is not uncommon for robots and automation to eliminate 30% or more of the human labor jobs that existed in the old plant. What will these workers do then? This realization makes it even more important that we find a method to discover the talents of people, for newly-discovered individual talents may be the only answer for future work opportunities.

There is more and more pressure to get this job of talent discovery done. In the beginning I knew it would help many people, now it appears most people may need it, and soon. I start to feel guilty when not working on talent, but I can't force my mind to be creative. The more confident I become that there is a solution, the greater I feel the pressure to find it. So far I have determined talent may be a combination of genetically-sponsored, efficient activities somehow synergistically enhanced.

Our conscious minds tend to form impressions of total activity events rather than the separate actions utilized in an activity. Currently, there is no study of human activities, which is difficult to believe with the varied research being done at colleges, universities, foundations and businesses.

We won't know how many different job tasks and human activities there are until they are catalogued and coded. Someone is going to have to design a method to catalogue and code job tasks and human activities, like the U.S. Department of Labor did with occupations. It is going to be costly and time consuming. Could the U.S. Department of Labor do it? They appear to know how and would benefit from such a project. Would government help finance private enterprise to do the project, as it did for the mapping of genes? I suspect private enterprise could code job tasks and human activities, and do it profitably because talent discovery could open up a whole new world of enterprise.

We still have the question of how efficient human activities are sponsored. How does synergism contribute to the efficiency of human activity groups, elevating them to a highly efficient talent status? How do we distinguish between positive and negative talent and bypass misinterpretations?

Having looked at efficiency and synergism we appear to be making some headway. Then there is the intrusion of genes, I wonder if genes will shed further light on talent discovery? What do I know of genes? This is becoming very complicated. I still feel a strong need to continue, but with talent discovery crossing over so many underdeveloped and highly scientific lines how can I possibly find a method of talent discovery? The thought that also crosses my mind is: if by the grace of God I do, who will believe me?

11

Genes
Spring 1991

*There are genes that govern a person's capacity to
develop physically and mentally in various ways,
there may be genes which govern and influence his
capacity to develop special abilities. However we
are just beginning to identify particular talent
genes and evolve theories as to how they work.*
AMRAM SCHEINFELD, *HEREDITY IN HUMANS*

The subject of genes made some of my pre-edit readers uneasy. Some felt I should eliminate the subject of genes completely, but I cannot. The thread of the talent discovery concept would have a gap that could not be explained and stop our progress. I have however, attempted to reduce the subject to simple language and bare necessity.

Synergism and Genes

What is this magic, this synergism? It does not help my search to say that the magic of a brilliant, talented performance "just is." An occupation is made up of job tasks consisting of human activities performed by actions sponsored by thought patterns. When these

103

highly efficient activities come together, their efficiency is modified and greatly expanded by synergistic action. How does synergism accomplish this?

The study of genetics is a difficult and incomplete science. However, if it will lead me to talent discovery then it is an area to study. Can genes somehow tie efficiency and synergism together?

Muscular action is sponsored by thought patterns activated by something. Genes must somehow be involved. Talent gene groupings could have been pre-programmed in all of us as standard equipment (like our fingers, toes, etc.). If this is true and everyone has genes that make talent ability available, why is it talent does not surface in everyone?

Talent and genes that we know so little about are going to be difficult to tie together. Nothing is happening. Let's set it aside for awhile.

Sedona, Arizona

Donna and I spent our 1991 spring vacation in the Sedona, Arizona area. We rented an adobe villa at the isolated Enchantment Resort on the side of a beautiful canyon. One night I drew a comfortable chair up to the fireplace, that had been lit for us while we were at dinner and opened one of the three books on genes I had brought along. Somewhere in these books I hoped to find a way to discover talent efficiency through genetics.

Currently, no one knows for sure how genes create, operate and control our mind and body; but there is research going on to answer these questions. Geneticists estimate there are 70,000 to 100,000 genes they are trying to sequence and map. Are there talent genes? If so, how do they operate and how do we find them?

I read that humans are made up and function according to the twenty-six chromosomes in the double helix of the genetic code. This code or blueprint dictates the biologic materials that must be manufactured for the body and brain to be created. This being true, isn't it logical all of the required genetic building blocks are present at birth and all require the same complement of basic genes? We could not come into existence without a complete complement of genes. Isn't it then possible that talent genes are built into everyone's genetic code at birth?

Let's re-run that: every human body has the same DNA structure; the same number of gene building blocks. If one genetic structure is capable of a high level of talent in a specific area then all genetic structures should be capable of a high level of talent in a specific area.

All humans may have the needed quantity of talent genes. The difference is that each of us has a different talent gene personality, as we have different facial features. All humans have faces and the same facial features, they are just arranged differently for each individual.

Late at night the words of the book I was reading started to blur, but my mind was active so I added more mesquite to the fire and let my mind wander. I began to suspect that our genetic structure knows the talents that are built into our system at birth. Our genes create our individuality (both physically and mentally), so genes may determine and have knowledge of the efficient activities that lead to our individual maximum talents. Individual talent may have always existed within us; we just have not developed a method of communicating with our genes to find our talents.

It is also logical that our genes carry out human activities by controlling our bodily actions. A single segment of our spinal cord controls the muscles it operates through several thousand moto-neurons. If moto-neurons are controlled by genes it requires some kind of genetic intelligence. If genes have intelligence, genes may know what combination of human activities and supporting actions are the most efficient in each individual. Do genes have a way of communicating this information to us?

Having added genes as a possible source of talent, I was now worried because I could not find any supportive research or information. One reference I did find that related genes to talent and ability was by Amram Scheinfeld:

> *There are genes that govern a person's capacity to*
> *develop physically and mentally in various ways.*
> *There may be genes which govern or influence his*
> *capacity to develop special abilities. However we*
> *are just beginning to identify particular talent*
> *genes and to evolve theories as to how they work.*
>
> HEREDITY IN HUMANS, 1971

. . . and another reference by Robert Shapiro:

> *Gregor for example might expect to find his*
> *vocational selection of engineering supported by*
> *the presence of genetic sequences associated with*
> *enhanced mathematical ability.*
>
> THE HUMAN BLUEPRINT, 1992

There it was, brought together by these two authors. I might be on the right track. Genes that govern. Genes and special abilities. Talent genes/genes in vocational selection. Genetic sequences/genes and enhanced ability.

This was not proof that all people have talent, but at least other learned people were thinking along the same lines, and I was not alone. When you delve into a highly-scientific and unknown field without formal education and by yourself draw highly technical conclusions . . . it is scary.

I finished reading the last of the three books on genetics while flying back to Milwaukee from Sedona. Soon after our return, I found genetics to be a popular subject on educational TV. I sent for a number of current tapes and CDs. The information didn't state talent genes existed; though several made vague reference to the possibility.

Human activity, however, became clearer to me as I started to understand how genes may be the source and control of human activity.

Genetic Activity

Since my wife enjoys baseball, we went to a Milwaukee Brewers/ Toronto Blue Jays game at the Milwaukee County Stadium. While watching the game, the action of the pitcher caught my attention. His shoulder, arm, elbow, hand, wrist and fingers . . . each performing an action worked together to support the activity of pitching the ball. He was able to become a major league pitcher because he was interested in the sport, he was willing to work and practice to perfect his throw, and he had the physical efficiency to excel.

Other people may want to become major league pitchers and they may be willing to work and practice but without the physical efficiency they can not succeed. No matter your environment or how hard you work and practice you will not become a star pitcher unless you have the efficient genetic capability to do so. The old adage "born, not made" may be true; and an indication talent genes could be present at birth.

Let's review. Throwing a baseball is an activity. The shoulder that controls the arm has a separate action, as do the elbow, wrist, hand and fingers when throwing.

Genes create a finger by building cells. Each created finger has certain actions it can perform. Geneticists indicate there are individual genes to instruct the cells to create bone, muscle, flesh, nail, and sensitive hair, all of which are a part of the finger. There must also be "cooperation" among the genes to coordinate the growth of the finger; genes can't create a fingernail before the flesh and bones are created. Again genes appear to have some form of intelligence.

Genes also maintain and repair the finger. Are these the same genes that created the finger? Some animals, insects, and sea life can recreate lost appendages; humans do not. Is it because our creative genes are different or have the genes become dormant? Could we wake-up these genes to re-grow an arm? Some geneticists have made reference to this possibility.

Back to the pitcher. He makes a mental decision to: put on the right equipment, study the hitting patterns of the batters, meet with the coach to establish the game plan, arrange signals with the catcher, react to the catcher's signals, and watch the base runners. On the mound a pitcher also decides how he will pitch to each particular batter, what kind of a ball he will throw, and how and where to throw it. These are mental thought patterns.

Pitching is a job task that involves a number of activities: throwing, catching, deciding what and how to throw to each individual batter, watching the catcher's signals, and watching the base runners. Each activity requires a series of physical actions and thought patterns. The process of throwing the ball is the key physical human activity requiring the most efficiency.

Gene Efficiency

Back to the pitcher. Is the talent efficiency present in his shoulder, arm, hand and fingers? Is that the difference between a major league pitcher and you and me? There are perhaps millions of cells and thousands of genes involved in creating and controlling the human shoulder, arm, wrist and fingers. What distinguishes a major league pitcher is a higher efficiency at pitching a baseball. It is not only his mental desire to succeed at pitching; his capability is determined by his physical make-up. The same is true of all sports. You might desire to become a professional skier, javelin thrower, long distance swimmer, sprinter, etc.; but your success is limited by your physical make-up. If your body is not capable of performing an activity efficiently your progress is limited. The human mind can only do so much to overcome physical limitations.

Throwing is an activity that involves the mind making a decision to throw. The pitcher had to make four key decisions: when, where, how and how fast to throw the ball. Each of these decisions required a different thought pattern. His body had to perform in at least four different action areas: the shoulder, arm, wrist and fingers. The raises another question: are the thousands of genes that control these four action areas involved in the pitching action? If so, is it the efficiency of the shoulder, arm, wrist and finger gene action groups working together efficiently that makes a talented pitcher? Or is there a single control gene in charge of the thousands of genes in each of the four action areas? If so, then the efficiency could be in the four highly efficient gene controllers working together.

Let's take this one step further. Is there a single control gene that controls the four efficient controller genes? If there are no control genes, then the thousands of genes involved in the four actions may have to operate in concert. Whatever way it is, there appears to be some kind of gene intelligence.

The conclusion drawn here is that pitching is a job task that utilizes human activities performed by physical action. Each action could be controlled by gene controllers or genes in concert.

Highly efficient gene groups working together result in a highly efficient activity, resulting in a superior pitching performance; the superior performance we call a talent capability.

Efficient activity and control genes may surface but the interplay of gene groupings that initiate interest and thus perform action remain unknown.

Throwing a different ball varies the activity. Throwing a football is different than throwing a basketball, baseball or softball.

We identify a dysfunctional gene for a known physical affliction by comparing the genes to the genes of a healthy person. The microscopic picture of a dysfunctional gene will appear abnormal when compared to a healthy person's genes. Other than this comparison, geneticists have not discovered a way to look at a gene and know what it is for. Thousands of junk genes that appear not to have a purpose are bypassed and not sequenced. Somewhere in the junk genes we may find clues to the talent genes.

Geneticists can recognize certain inherited defective genes and correct or replace them. Through genetic research, we are now able to predict medical problems for members of a family who share the same defective genes. Some traits, such as our physical makeup, are fixed. Our action patterns are physically fixed but are subject to learning and control. Our endless neuron thinking patterns, although influenced by experience may also be subject to learning and control may not be fixed, and they too may have a personality of their own.

The workings of efficient genes and efficient gene groups resulting in talented activities are unknown to us. However, because of the great number of genes and vast number of potential gene combinations, it is reasonable to assume that each one of us has combinations of efficient gene groups that are particular to us.

It is also reasonable to assume each individual has a different combination of highly efficient human activities (or maximum talent capabilities) that can fit best in one or more of the 40,000 occupations.

Finally, in the vast number of efficient human activity combinations (known as talent) there is one combination of activities that each individual can do better than any other combination of activities; and probably better than any other individual.

Each of you has a valuable unknown talent, one that is exclusively yours; and if there is a way to find it you have found your most valuable asset.

> *"The popular belief that most people are not very*
> *smart is far more an obstacle to developing genius*
> *than anything of a practical nature."*
>
> PETER KLINE, *THE EVERYDAY GENIUS*

Why isn't everyone desperately searching for hidden talent? Because we were not brought up or educated to believe everyone has talent and therefore we are not looking for it. Logic and evidence indicates that every individual has a unique built-in maximum talent capability.

The efficiency of genes appears to answer the question of how activities become efficient; though I still have the problem of how synergism modifies and elevates combinations of efficient and compatible activities to talent. These are the deductions on genes so far:

+ Genes are responsible for human construction and body maintenance, therefore genes may control human activity.
+ Efficient genes in combination may sponsor efficient actions resulting in efficient human activity.
+ Combinations of efficient and compatible human activities result in talent.
+ Qualified talent results in maximum talent capability.

To use maximum talent capabilities we will have to catalogue and code job tasks and human activities. Our objective is to find individuals with the maximum talent capabilities that best match the over 40,000 occupations.

We have these unanswered questions. The source of efficiency and synergism appears to be found; but how do efficient and qualified activity groups utilize synergism to become maximum talent capabilities?

Is there a way to distinguish between positive and negative talent? Is there a way to qualify activities as to physical and mental health? Is there a way to bypass a person's misconceptions that result in misinterpretations? Is there a way to penetrate the genetic structure or the brain to find an individual's most efficient activities?

Assuming we find the answers to these questions, how do we apply maximum talent capabilities to certain occupations where these talents can best be used?

These are clear objectives; although they seem so formidable as to be almost impossible to obtain. I do not feel qualified to accomplish all of these things. I should stop right now, forget the whole idea, toss it in the garbage and end the anxiety. I could then complete the novels I enjoy writing without this constant interruption and irritation. But no, it won't let me go; even though I know this area is way beyond my capability. At night my subconscious mind, or that know-it-all Henry, will not let me rest. Henry is terribly pushy.

(Upon editing this manuscript, I became conscious of how Henry might appear to some readers: "this guy is kind of weird, talking to himself." However, while writing this book, I have tried to be as honest as possible on how this whole scenario happened, and leaving Henry out of my story would be less than honest.) Was Henry a figment of my imagination?

I then began to wonder if other people have had the same experience; I found many have. Robert Louis Stevenson, Charles Dickens, W.M. Thackeray, John Keats, George Eliot, Johann Von Goethe, Thomas Alva Edison and Albert Einstein all referred to some kind of mysterious and outside source of help in their work and in finding solutions.

Keats said his writing "must have come by chance or magic" or "something given to him." Dickens said when he sat down to write "some beneficent power" came to him. And, author James Clavell's novel *Gai-Jin* is dedicated:

> *This novel is for you, whoever you are, with deep*
> *appreciation . . . for without you, the writer part of*
> *me would not exist.*

At first, his comment puzzled me. Did he really mean what it implied? But then I knew; for my someone (Henry) keeps pushing and helping me too, for my own good.

We do not know how or why ideas come to people, it is humbling and it should be. Did the talent discovery concept enter my thoughts because my background of exposure, work and interests were closest to a possible talent discovery method?

Somehow, some of us perceive that we are not alone or could it be that when we approach our natural talent areas we somehow activate an internal help or intelligence? I do not have the answer for this question, but I do know I need all the help I can get to continue in this growing and ever more complicated entanglement that must be sorted out to resolve the talent discovery issue.

12

Talent Genetics
Summer 1991

*The traces of this facilitation of the evolution of
intelligence may still be detectable in the genes.
Understanding them may point the way toward
our own next intellectual advance which we will
surely take just as soon as we understand
how to accomplish it.*
CHRISTOPHER WILLS, *THE WISDOM OF THE GENES*

I try to visualize where my research has taken me and where I am
being led. Do I have a clear picture? Why am I approaching
talent in this particular way? Are there other ways to find what
talent is? Random words and thoughts seem to lead me on. Now I
am in unknown territory, making too many assumptions about how
genes work. I do not have an organized approach. I may need some
professional help to see if there is a more practical approach.

"Who says it has to be practical?"

"Henry? Where have you been?"

"Around."

"Henry I don't know if you can help. I feel discouraged and way
over my head."

"You're not the first discouraged person who made it."

"I don't know where to start," I said.

"You'll find a way."

"How can you be so sure?"

"I know you."

"I don't know what you mean. Henry, can you explain to me who you really are?"

"I'm your mentor."

"My what?"

"Your mentor, helper, conscious, sometimes subconscious, call me what you will. You need me, whoever you think I am," continues Henry.

"Are you the one who tells me what I should not do?" I query.

"Could be."

"If I recall you've been wrong a few times," I challenge.

"So who's perfect?"

"Are you the one who put all these stories in my head?"

"What do you think?"

"I don't know what to think."

"You asked for professional help?"

"You're a professional?" I ask.

"Eh? . . . in a way. Back to your problem. What's your question?"

"As an example, my mind throws out this word synergistic as a vehicle to enhance an efficient and compatible group of activities that become a maxtalability. Why does it throw this word out without supporting evidence?"

"Why do you think?"

"Well, I suppose it could be up to me to find how genes play a part in synergism," I reply.

"Was that so difficult?"

"Well . . . no, but I'm not qualified to do that. It's way over my head."

"The human mind gets muddled. That's why you need me to raise questions and nudge you on a little; so you keep up confidence in what you're doing. You're in virgin territory; and as you said, 'That's a little scary for a neophyte.' Established technical methods may not apply. Look back and see how far you've come," Henry encouraged. "You're tying the parts together very well. Relax, you're doing all right."

"But by now the direction should start to clear. There are more questions than ever. I think I know the direction, but we ought to put it into words so we can sit back and analyze it."

"Okay. What have you been doing?"

"I have been taking talent apart and analyzing it piece by piece and trying to follow the thread of why and how it operates to become a maxtalability," I explain.

"Why?"

"To find out what talent is."

"Why?"

"To see how it works."

"Why?"

"Let's see. So somehow in this process of taking talent apart we can find a way or method to discover an individual's maximum talent capability."

"Are you on that track?" Henry asks.

"I seem to be making some progress."

"That's not all bad. So what do you need me for?" Blip.

There he goes again. Every time he leaves me up in the air with my head buzzing. Well maybe I am on the right track.

Back to Genes

It is not my intention to imply that I am a genetic expert. Having read and researched books and publications, and watched numerous videos, one fact is obvious: little is known about genes, especially in the area of intelligence, and how genes react, control and cooperate.

Genes remind me of tiny individuals. They live, take protein nourishment, create, control, act, react, repair, replace, mutate, make decisions, work individually or in groups.

They know what time it is; they become dormant and then wake again. Maybe genes have their own "computer" to do their work or do they use the brain for a computer? (That's an interesting thought.) Genes are strange little individuals, each working in different combinations to create different humans, and their actions, abilities and personalities.

Specific genes have the same function in every body; yet each gene may have its own personality. As individuals we are affected by what we eat and how our bodies utilize nourishment.

The same appears to be true of a gene and how it utilizes proteins. Genes are subject to deficiencies; as evidenced by the discovery of weak or dysfunctional genes. It therefore follows that genes may have different levels of efficiency. If we can find weak and dysfunctional genes, which are low efficiency genes, then there must be high efficiency genes that would enhance human activities.

Our genes evidently built us, and they know what is acceptable to our health and what we can do best. Genes probably know what our individual highest capabilities are; but they are not telling us.

Why don't we know? Perhaps humans have not paid enough attention to what we are. Genes know about and have controlled commonly used human activities since the beginning of humanity.

It appears that every individual was created from the same basic genetic blueprint. To genes, continued advances in technology may be foreign to them; therefore to find an individual's talent we need to find a way to communicate with genes on their own level.

Perhaps this is what talent discovery is set out to accomplish: to find a way to communicate through a language genes know all about ... human activity.

Genes created eons ago evidently have no knowledge of activities involved in today's technologies. Genes may not know what occupations are; they were not created to practice law, biochemistry or auto mechanics. Genes may be more familiar with the human activities involved in hunting, foraging for food and other survival activities.

Exposed long enough genes may mutate and adapt to a techno-logical environment. It may take eons, how would we know?

We know the human brain is adaptable and has unused capac-ity; but maybe our genes are more anchored in time.

Other than replacing or artificially forcing genes to adapt, thereby permanently changing us, there does not appear to be a way to force genes to know the requirements of today's highly- technical occupa-tions.

This is what I'm getting at: genes do not know what specific occupations are but they must know human activities that make up job tasks and occupations. How can we use this fact? I haven't the vaguest idea. Let's put that on hold for awhile.

Motivation

If we build a hundred different robots exactly alike they will all perform at the same efficiency level. One hundred individuals would not do the same work at the same efficiency level, even though all people are designed from the same genetic blueprint. A robot is not mentally influenced by action, activity or talent; as individuals are. A hundred people will not perform the same because each of their genetic structures has a different interest and preference/abhorrence personality of its own. Each individual has a different set of inter-ests that contributes to a different talent personality.

Interest may influence the efficiency performance of talent. This may be done by the part of the brain that controls the level of motivational energy released for a particular interest. The more a particular activity is acceptable, challenging or enjoyable to the brain the more motivational energy the brain may release. If the brain, through repetition, starts to find an interest boring or lacking in challenge, the brain may simply shut down motivation.

Motivation may be similar to a generator in an automobile en-gine: when the generator stops the auto runs on the battery alone as long as it can, then dies. When the brain loses interest, motivation cuts out and activity runs as long as it can, then it runs out of power. The greater the interest, the greater the motivation the brain allows to become available.

Geneticists tell us that genes need certain proteins to function and stay healthy. This brings us back to the question of the efficiency of individual genes and gene groups. Does the brain also influence genes through a similar motivation method by providing or withholding the level of protein nourishment that the genes need?

Is the mind selfish in its own enjoyment of preferred interests or are its decisions based on what is good for the body or the body's capability?

Genius-Genes

A great pianist, such as Vladmir Horowitz, can express such beauty during a performance as to bring tears to one's eyes. Many people can play the piano; few can equal Horowitz. Other people can dedicate as much time and effort to playing the piano as Horowitz; yet they will not reach the level of Horowitz's talent. What is the difference? Do highly talented people have some mystical gift that is not visible?

I suspect that the difference is in the efficiency of the gene grouping. Horowitz's gene grouping in the human activities required to play the piano are just that much more efficient. This sounds very cold and impersonal, but really nothing has changed, it is just a different way of looking at a talent.

All of us have the necessary complement of genes. Remember our baseball pitcher. If our pitcher and Mr. Horowitz have efficient gene capability; then it could be that each of us has our own individual grouping of genes that are more efficient than any other of our individual gene groups. Genes continue to be the activity efficiency source.

Interest in a particular activity cannot force efficient performance if the body cannot perform the required physical activity in an efficient manner. Physical activity cannot perform over a long period of time if the mind grows tired or bored with the activity.

Genetic efficiency results in what we call talent that is subject to other bodily interpretations. To find an individual's maxtalability, the physical, and mental gene groups must find the activity not only preferable but highly acceptable.

Fingerprints/Genes

Everyone requires a full complement of genes to build their fingerprint ridges with cells. There are evidently enough fingerprint gene cell combinations created so no two set of fingerprints are ever completely alike. Because of the infinite number of potential gene combinations it is also unlikely that two individuals (living or who have ever lived) have the same genetic talent personality. The combination potentials of gene groups consisting of 70,000 to 100,000 genes are certainly much more diverse than fingerprints. All people must have different gene combinations that result in talent.

In this vast combination of genes, activities, job tasks and occupations, there may never be an efficient grouping of talent genes that matches an individual with an occupation perfectly. Our objective should be to find one or more occupations that match an individual as closely as possible; that would be their maximum talent capability. This discovery would take us out of the occupation wilderness we have been wandering in.

I know more about genes than I did before but that knowledge is of little help. Most of my questions remain unanswered. We are what we are. The powers that be can't change us without tampering with our genes; **and that alternative is not acceptable.** We have to find the maxtalability in each individual before gene tampering becomes that alternative.

Research of genes provides additional evidence as to the efficiency of genes resulting in talent. However, I still have to find the missing link on how synergism elevates combinations of efficient activities to maximum talent capabilities. To restate my gene deductions:

+ Genes are responsible for human construction, body maintenance and individuality; therefore genes may control human activity through actions.

+ Efficient genes result in efficient actions and therefore efficient human activities.

+ Compatible combinations of efficient human activities and actions result in talent.

+ Qualified talents are maximum talent capabilities that can be applied to one or more of the over 40,000 known occupations.

Our objective remains to apply an individual's maximum talent capabilities to the best occupations possible. These questions remain unanswered:

+ Is there a way to distinguish between positive and negative talent?

+ Is there a way to qualify activities as to physical, mental and emotional health?

+ Is there a way to bypass a person's misconceptions that result in misinterpretations?

+ Is there a way to penetrate the genetic structure or the brain to find an individual's most efficient activities?

If we find these answers, how do efficient and qualified activity and action groups utilize synergism to become maximum talent capabilities?

Assuming we find these answers, how do we apply maximum talent capabilities to occupations where these talents can be best used? To do this we are required to find a way to catalogue and code job tasks, human activities and actions.

Although it appears logical that genes play an important part in efficiency no important breakthroughs have been made. As I feared, the problems and questions continue to expand and we are starting to bog down. This causes me concern and anxiety, for every day I am more aware of how much better the lives of people would be if they knew and had the use of their best natural abilities.

13

Human Activity-Synergism
August 1991

...geneticists have speculated about what talent might be...when it comes to more complex human activities...we are woefully ignorant about the genetic component and its phenotypical expression...rather than being related to a specific gene or small set of genes, any complex trait reflects many genes.
HOWARD GARDNER, FRAMES OF MIND

I suspect talent gene control originates in the brain but I do not know how synergism elevates job tasks, activities and actions to talent status. It appears to be necessary to first understand how synergism works its magic. How can I bridge the gap between efficient genes and maximum talent? I need a simple explanation; if there is one. I don't have the slightest idea how to approach this subject. I need help!

"Henry at your service."

"Henry, you know anything about synergism and talent?" I ask.

"You do."

"How so?"

"Took some talent to build your companies, going up against Fortune 500 companies in highly competitive markets with no capital."

"I certainly don't feel talented."

"Bashful, huh? Come on, what were your talents?"

"Well . . . let me think. I worked hard selecting, training and leading the right people . . . and . . . maybe promotion, selling, marketing, creating things, solving problems."

"That's quite a string of efficient talents working together; but certainly needed to build companies."

"That does not tell me what talent is or how it is elevated to maximum talent capability status," I challenged.

"How did you find talent in yourself?"

"A wide range of hands-on exposure, responsibilities and opportunities, I guess."

"So expose other people."

"Cm'on Henry. There is no way everyone can have the number of different jobs and exposures that I did."

"If, as you suspect, everyone has maximum talent capabilities, then they must exist. That which exists can be found. Find another way."

"What other way could there be to find how synergism elevates job tasks, activities and actions to maxtalability status to prove everyone could have maximum talent capabilities?"

"You and your circle of talents working together in the round created some kind of a synergism. You have to be the clue. See ya."
Blip.

Just like that, he's gone again. As usual Henry won't answer questions on the subject. I wonder what he meant by that "circle of talents" and "I am it." I don't feel very talented now and I don't know what he's talking about.

Jasper, Canada-1991

Donna and I spent our fall vacation in the northwestern part of the United States and Canada. Donna had not seen Washington or

Oregon and had always wanted to take a scenic train trip, I wanted to see Alberta Canada, so we tied the three together. In September 1991, we flew to Seattle. We spent two nights at the Salishan Lodge on the ocean in Gleneden Beach, Oregon; then we drove up to Vancouver, Canada and stayed at the beautiful Pan Pacific Hotel.

After checking in and cleaning up I went down to the Pan Pacific Hotel Cascades Lounge bar in advance of Donna to hold one of the cocktail tables overlooking the scenic Burrard Inlet.

I sat half facing the harbor and occasionally glancing over to the lobby . . . the way Donna would have to enter the lounge. As I sat there, I listened to the soft background music of Glen Miller's *String of Pearls*. What a beautiful and original piece of music. A thought crossed my mind . . . string of pearls?

Something was coming together about talent and synergism. I had the thought for a brief moment, when something alerted me. I turned and there Donna stood just outside the bar in the hotel lobby. She saw me, gave me a glorious smile and walked quickly towards me; slightly breezy with head held high. I told her how beautiful and youthful she appeared; but she just laughed lightly and with a wave of her hand said. "Oh, you're just imagining things."

No way. She is a lovely woman with many great qualities. How lucky can a guy get?

The loss of that thought preyed on my mind. I had to find some way to get it back.

The next afternoon we boarded the night train to Jasper in Alberta, Canada. We experienced a beautiful mountain and wilderness ride with fine dining in the vintage dining car. I was thinking about the 1954 movie The Glen Miller Story, when Glen Miller's orchestra first played *The String of Pearls* his wife was sitting in the audience. After the music he gave her a real string of pearls. I was trying to re-enact the scene to revive my lost thought; with no success.

Mid-afternoon I took a nap with the track rumbling below. When I awoke . . . there it was, the fleeting thought. I was not looking for a mixed circle of job tasks, activities and actions strung together to make a talent, but rather a circle made up of matched, efficient, and compatible human activities—like a string of perfectly matched pearls!

It can't be only actions because actions carry out activities, and it can't be job tasks because they break down into activities and are a step removed from actions. Human activities relate to both job tasks and actions. It is a set of efficient human activities that compliment each other; forming a circle of talent. Let me cite another example: When a circle is completed it gains added strength and efficiency. One strand of a chain can withstand only so much pull. Connect the strand into a continuous circle and you have two strands that will withstand more force than the single strand. That is a form of synergism.

The same circle principle is used in an electric motor. An armature turns in a magnetic field circle of matched magnets, strung together by copper wire. When the magnets (matched) and in a circle are given a start, in a few seconds the armature is revolving thousands of revolutions a minute creating substantial electrical power. That is real synergism. If the magnets are not matched the motor would not turn at all. That could be the way a circle of efficient activities works; they complement each other like the magnets and create a field of high talent. A circle of efficient activities allows each activity to react to all the other efficient activities in the circle and that creates an energy field that enhances ability.

Now I think I understand how and why a circle of synergism works; but is it clear to you? I need help with this.

"Thought I already helped with this."

"Hi, Henry. I know but I need to develop a clearer explanation of how synergism works in a circle of efficient human activities."

"I gave you 'round.' "

"Well yes, I've got that; the string of pearls. The matched human activities in a circle that work upon each other creating a synergistic field, but how? I need a clearer explanation."

"String of pearls, heh, heh, that's really reaching. Not bad; but kind of corny," chuckled Henry.

"Corny?"

"Well the idea got you there; but forget it. Back to business. I gave you 'round.' It is not my job to spell it out for you. Oh well, under what circumstances did you use round in your business to utilize talent for business objectives?"

"Let me think," I said.

"Yeah, you do that." Blip.

"Henry?!" He's gone again. Let's see . . . in the round? Oh sure, now I know. In our company whenever we had a problem, those responsible and those showing talent or interest in that particular problem were invited into my office for a round table discussion to find ways to solve the problem. This was done in the round purposely because people compliment each other. As people talk and share ideas they stimulate each other, ask questions, explore possibilities, and develop thoughts and solutions.

It is done in the round to have the advantage of seeing every one's expressions. Nonverbal cues, such as facial expression, body language, hand gesture, direction of gaze, and eye contact are often a more accurate and truthful expression than words. Sometimes people can express and accentuate thoughts or ideas with body language more efficiently. A person can almost see the energy and vibration sparks fly in the air as ideas combine, collide, unfold and develop. This is pure synergism. This kind of round table process is widely used by businesses.

The same thing happens in an individual's mind when the individual has the use of a circle of efficient human activities of common dedication. When a person is interested in something, the attention or motivation voltage in the neurons of the brain accelerate. Efficient activities bounce back and forth against each other in the neurons of the brain, opening up more and more neuron circuits. This strong energy field opens doors wide, tapping great reserves of innovation, creativity and problem solving.

This is how the brain could develop synergism. However if there is even one unmatched magnet the electric motor will not run. One activity out of sync, inefficient or negative mixed in the circle of efficient activities and it may not create a synergistic field. All the necessary efficient and compatible human activities must be present for synergism to spawn maximum talent capabilities.

With so many different human activities, a matched set of efficient human activities needed to create a maxtalability is not going to be easy to find. A circle of efficient human activities reminds me of dealing a deck of cards. The chance of four people each ending up with a single suit of thirteen cards is in the millions. There are only fifty-two cards but there are untold thousands of human activities in the 40,000 occupations. The chance of individuals discovering a compatible combination of their most efficient activities by accident or on purpose, without some shortcut method, must be incalculable. That may be why scientists and educators have not been looking for or are able to find talents. If we could somehow find an individual's combination of efficient human activities we might uncover the secret to finding an individual's talents.

Glen Miller's *String of Pearls* helped clear up a complicated step. Efficient activities working together picks up synergism and the result is talent. Important headway was made, now perhaps I could relax and enjoy the rest of the trip.

On our return trip to Milwaukee I was bothered by something about synergism and how it organizes those complimentary efficient human activities into a talent. There appeared to be a gap, something was missing. The result of synergism is a high level of creativity and problem solving in a particular talent area. That is when the word intelligence popped into my mind?

In Milwaukee our plane hit the runway rather hard and the bump must have jarred my mind, for the answer came to me. The true source of creativity and problem solving does not come from talent, talent is the result. Could it be the application of intelligence to the matched human activities? That seems too obvious and simple.

When synergism takes place, could it be enhanced by opening the door to creative and problem solving intelligence. Talent results in creativity and problem solving . . . and intelligence does the work. How very interesting. Thus synergism resulting in talent is the result of intelligence applied to efficient and qualified human activities. This does not change the gene concept but recognizes the role intelligence plays, and it closes an important gap. The mind opens the door to the wealth of intelligence an individual possesses, and that is what modifies and enhances the efficient and compatible combination of human activities to talent status.

This being and acceptable answer, we know more now than we did before. Headway has been made by establishing how matched efficient and compatible activities become synergistic by drawing on intelligence resulting in maximum talent capability; yet other questions remain:

+ Is there a way to distinguish between positive and negative talent?
+ How do we qualify activities to eliminate those that are stressful and unhealthy?
+ How do we bypass the influence of work and occupational misconceptions to allow an individual free and clear appraisal of an activity by the mind?
+ Is there a way to penetrate the genetic structure or the brain to find an individual's most efficient activities? Assuming we find these answers how do we apply talents to occupations where these talents can best be used?

To do this we are required to find a way to catalogue and code job tasks and human activities. I have no idea which problem will be easiest to work on next, they all look formidable. At this juncture there are no clues that I can recognize. Obviously to penetrate the genetic structure or brain to find maximum talent capabilities would be logical, but I have no idea where to start or how that can be accomplished.

Months go by. Fall fades into winter without a single new thought or idea coming to me. My confidence level is very low. It looks like discovering talent was just a fantasy. It would be so very wonderful for all humans; but, now it appears to be fading into the realm of impossible dreams.

14

Senses That Judge
December 1992

*Current research in physiology suggests that the
mind doesn't dwell in the brain but travels the
whole body on caravans of hormone and enzyme,
busily making sense of the compound wonders we
catalogue as touch, taste, smell,
hearing and vision.*
DIANE ACKERMAN, *A NATURAL HISTORY OF THE SENSES*

On Christmas night as I listened to a church choir on TV, attempting to hold onto Christmas music just a little longer, a news announcer came on and said: "On this night there are wars going on all over the world. Did you know that in wars there are more civilian casualties, including children, than soldier casualties? All of our prayers have not diminished war. For many people there is no peace on earth."

How can we stop war? Who are these people making wars? Why do they do it? Some people seek freedom through insurrection but most war-mongers appear to be driven by ambition, greed and the need for personal identity. Could any of those people, including the ranks of followers, find a safer and more rewarding way of expending their energies? What if they discovered their hidden talents? Something they really cared about? Would a talented violinist join an army when he might lose the use of his hand? If war followers found another interest of importance to them would war instigators have a more difficult time making war? Would talent discovery be of value in bringing peace to earth?

This Christmas night I prayed that a way to discover individual talent would be found. There are so many seemingly impossible problems left to solve on the way to talent discovery that I am overwhelmed. Perhaps I am not the person to do this; but again, who else believes it exists?

There is no doubt that talent discovery is vital to the future of all people. If, through talent discovery, individuals work in professions that compliment their health and abilities they will have a much greater chance for success and happiness.

The morning after Christmas I woke up with the word "senses" running through my mind, as though it was all-important.

My subconscious must have been busy last night. So here I go again. Senses? Well, that's interesting. I might be able to work with the senses. They are responsive to activities. Maybe senses are the qualifying factor I am looking for? How can senses help?

Let's analyze senses.

Senses are safeguards that protect us against activities which can potentially harm us physically and mentally. Our brain may be interested in an activity but if our senses find the occupation, task or activity offensive then before we can continue the activity, our brain must override our senses. So if the senses turn thumbs down on an activity the senses are not going to cooperate; they will cause friction, frustration and stress. Our sense personality can have built-in likes, dislikes or indifference for the most minor feelings or touches. To quote Diane Ackerman:

> ...Research suggests that, though there are four
> main types of receptors, there are many others
> along a wide spectrum of response. After all our
> palette of feelings through touch is more elaborate

than hot, cold, pain and pressure. Many touch
receptors combine to produce what we call a
twinge. Consider all the varieties of pain,
irritation, abrasion; and all the textures of lick, pat,
wipe, fondle, knead; all the prickling, bruising,
tingling, brushing, scratching, banging, fumbling,
kissing nudging.

In recent years researchers have studied the workings of smell, touch, taste, hearing and vision. Dr. Gordon Shepard, a Yale University professor of neurobiology, indicates that there may be as many as twenty distinct senses. Balance for example would be important to a high wire artist or a high rise construction worker.

There are over 50 different human emotions between pleasure and displeasure; our exposure and experiences can tilt the balance either way. Our interest in emotions that are truthful . . . those which have not been distorted may help lead us to a person's maximum and even qualified talent. We could refer to these emotions as "awakening emotions" since they describe when an individual is exposed to something that inspires him/her to a motivation-supported response. We also have to distinguish between emotions that appeal to bodily appetites rather than intellectual interests. And we might also have to consider that different people have different levels of expression.

It would appear that memory and instinct would have different responses. Would an instinct response have a closer relation to our best capabilities?

Human activity efficiency is affected by an individual's sensitivity to activities, people and things. The flight simulator used to test and train jet pilots, in which the pilot sees, touches, feels and hears the experience, is so vivid the test can eliminate people whose senses cannot handle the experience. The first flight simulators were so real that even experienced pilots came out of the unit sweating and trembling so much that a doctor was needed on site.

The senses remember. They remind an individual if a previously encountered activity was pleasant, unpleasant or offensive.

Thought patterns of the mind are also influenced by memory. The senses are an impressionable and important judge of things experienced, as they pass their decisions on to the mind. To be an efficient activity the cooperation of the senses would be needed.

The senses appear to be based in the primitive or self defense-preservation area of the brain. This portion of the brain was created to help maintain and protect us.

The brain tells us what it wants to do, the body tells us if we can, and the senses tell us if they will support an activity. Thought patterns, physical motions, and sense interpretations make up what we may refer to as the forces that initiate, control and qualify human activities.

Could there be a common intelligence that connects the physical body, mind and senses? These areas need each other to function.

Gene efficiency could drop if the human senses find an activity unpleasant. As an example: tasting (as in wine tasting), hearing (as in music), seeing (as in art) and touching (as in fabric selection). An individual who likes a certain activity will find the efficiency of an activity is affected when smell is an important factor. Each of our senses expresses a judgment: either pleasant, indifferent or unpleasant. Scientists indicate that this judgment is exercised through electrical impulses.

> *Each of the senses works in a similar way,*
> *converting a particular type of chemical,*
> *mechanical or electromagnetic energy into*
> *electrical impulses that are passed along to the*
> *brain for interpretation.*
>
> ROBERT RIVILIN AND KAREN GRAVELLE,
> *DECIPHERING THE SENSES*

Every individual has their own sense personality, which is why people may react differently to the same thing. I have been looking for a way to communicate with the brain to qualify talents; what better way than through the senses? But there is a problem. In a search for talent the senses, like the mind could not be familiar with the actions, activities and job tasks of 40,000 occupations to make a valid judgment. Is there a way to get around this problem?

Let's summarize the process: one part of the brain develops an interest so it initiates either mental and/or physical action. When physical action is required, the physical body indicates if it can, and to what extent it wants to, perform the activity as required. The senses either accept or reject the activity the brain, with the body's support, has decided to perform.

The brain may have it's own non-physical sensory system. as an example "boredom." After an interest has passed the physical and sense qualifications, another part of the brain decides if the thought patterns are acceptable, challenging and for how long of a time it will find it so. A long span could be an occupation, a short span a hobby or recreation.

If the senses do not approve it would be difficult for an efficient set of activities to become a maxtalability; the senses will drag their feet thus eliminating the efficiency of the activity. Could the brain's sensory system exercise its judgment by having its hand on the throttle control of available motivation?

Can we bypass the misconception experience memory of both the mind and the senses? They can misinterpret or react falsely to occupations, job tasks and activities. Although we may not have been bitten by a snake our senses will react differently to a harmless snake or a rabbit. We cannot expect an honest reaction to occupations or activities from the senses if we do not bypass misconceptions; misconceptions that come from sources such as:

1. We have been exposed to fiction through reading, radio, plays and TV. Facts about occupations are distorted or slanted

to accommodate a story. With this limited experience memory our minds cannot know the difference.

2. We have been exposed to occupations that may or may not appeal to us because of one brief experience. That experience may not have been a fair exposure to an occupation.

3. We are influenced by how other people describe their experiences and what details they tell us. No two people can feel or describe an occupation in the same way. In description people express how they individually interpret or feel about a subject.

4. We are influenced by people in positions of respect who tell or show us what they want us to know rather than what is.

5. Our senses are responsive to unshakable facts stored in the brain that are often found not to be as was previously thought. Many are not true at all. We learn as facts change and new ideas come forth.

Misconceptions are a problem that we will have to face. If not for misconceptions the conscious mind may be able tell us more about our abilities. The question remains: How do we bypass the influence of work and occupational misconceptions to allow an individual free and clear appraisal of an activity by the mind?

The detour provided by the senses was nothing but a tease; providing some help in qualification but leaving small hope of solving the rest of the problems, especially the issue of penetrating the brain.

15

Common Denominator
Spring 1993

*In a high wage information economy, people are
paid for what is unique to them...their intelligence
and creativity, not their collective brawn.*
JOHN NAISBITT & PATRICIA ABURDENE, MEGATRENDS 2000

What is the subconscious? Does it take over when the conscious mind is asleep? It appears that way to me. My conscious mind is more influenced by what I have seen, read, heard and experienced. The subconscious mind apparently knows what the conscious knows; in addition my subconscious is more imaginative and works longer and harder at creating and problem solving.

I look to my subconscious for help in solving problems when I sleep. Although I had little hope of ever penetrating the brain, I would occasionally review the talent discovery problems to be solved in chronological order before I went to sleep. Sometimes in the middle of the night I am suddenly awakened with an idea and I quickly write it down because in the morning when I wake-up it will most likely be gone. I have lost or delayed many items of value because I was too tired to get up during the night, thinking I would remember in the morning.

In the morning I relax in bed and let whatever my subconscious has come up with during the night flow across my conscious mind. Some mornings the subconscious asks questions, suggests key words or research that might lead to answers. Sometimes there is nothing; other times the subconscious prefers to work on personal, family or business problems. The subconscious mind is quite independent. I can ask for help from my subconscious mind but I can't demand it, otherwise it will turn off.

I find the subconscious is more of a computer problem solver; more logical and truthful. I often wonder if Henry is involved in my subconscious.

One night I asked my subconscious to work on a way to familiarize the brain with 40,000 occupations and their job tasks, activities and actions. The next morning "human activity" returns to haunt me again. What is that sneaky subconscious doing now? Why human activity? We have already established human activity is the physical and mental activities we engage in all day long. Complementary efficient activities working together have the benefit of synergism that results in qualified talent or maximum talent capabilities.

How could human activity help to compare maximum talent capabilities to 40,000 occupations? To submit an individual to an honest picture of what each of the 40,000 occupations consist of, we would have to create a visual of each occupation, broken down into job tasks, human activities, and actions. We would end up with a visual library of occupations, job tasks, human activities. How would that help?

Cataloguing, coding and creating visuals, although time-consuming and expensive, would bring us closer to understanding and experiencing job tasks, activities and actions.

People could scroll through a computerized visual library. Again, this would be time-consuming but would be of help in acquainting people with a great span of occupations and their makeup. In a rudimentary way, when I had people do the "Getting to Know You" job task exercise, they were accomplishing a similar task. Most people found the exercise enlightening and valuable.

The government-sponsored Genome Project is committed to mapping genes, why not map job tasks, human activities and actions? Most of the present benefit of the Genome project is in the gene repair of people with dysfunctional genes as well as development and production of drugs to treat dysfunctional genes and other health problems. The discovery of talent activity genes would be a positive benefit to everyone.

How do we create a visual library of the job tasks and human activities involved in 40,000 occupations? Is there a shortcut? I was stymied again and set the problems of talent aside.

Life Planning

I decided to organize material I had been accumulating to write a book on life planning, or how to plan your life at any age. I had been working on this book for more than twenty years. Life planning should be taught in school and it can be done. People spend more time planning a weekend than they do planning their lives. Life planning provides an individual with direction, a reason for doing the right things that fit and a reason for not doing wrong things that don't fit.

Life plans are subject to change. That's all right, every thing in life is subject to change. A plan that is changeable is better than no plan. If you don't have a target, how can you practice and become proficient at shooting at targets (the goals and objectives of life)?

Every time I tried to write about life planning I was led back to talent. If people knew their talents they would have a stronger and more permanent foundation on which to plan their lives. So I am right back where I started. What was that all about?

Something Simple

I still don't know what my subconscious mind thought was so important about human activity. Somehow, I had to get into the brain. (I don't mean surgically, rather I need to find a way to use what the brain knows about it's ability.)

To find an individual's most efficient maximum talent capabilities we must bypass the misinterpretations of the mind and senses. If I could solve this problem, how do we then apply maximum talent capabilities to occupations where they can best be used? Why is my subconscious pushing human activity. I don't see the connection; guess I need help with this?

"You're not getting very far."

"Henry, tell me, what am I supposed to do with human activity?" I ask.

"Think!"

"I suppose you know the answers. They are not that simple."

"Say that again, son."

"It's not that simple. So?"

"Say that again."

"Hmm. Simple?? What do you mean?"

"Look son, you're looking for a complicated scientific answer. In the future people may get into the brain through complicated means to find talent, but not in this era," Henry replied.

"You mean a simple answer. It had better be. I'm not good at complicated things and people don't want or won't use complicated things."

"Who says? Look at the number of complicated home computers there are today. People don't know how the things work but they use them. Don't loose heart, stay with it. You're doing okay, and remember . . . if you can help people find new talents and help millions more in their careers, that's a lot of people you will have helped. That's pretty good."

"I know. So how do I find a simple answer?" I ask.

"You will, just stop thinking it's complicated. Let your mind free to consider what you already know."

"Are you suggesting that I already have an answer to one of these problems?"

"Could be."

"Henry, are you part of my self-conscious that works in my head at night?"

"Enough, you got your help." Blip.

He's gone again. Every time he interferes my head buzzes. Back to the problem. Something simple that I already know about. We know senses can qualify human activities as to exposure by positive, indifference or negative response. Let's try familiarizing the senses with 40,000 occupations in terms of human activities my subconscious is pushing.

To find maximum talent capabilities, ideal occupations that fit an individual well, an individual would have to work hands-on at each of 40,000 or more known occupations. Spending sufficient time at each of the 40,000 occupations to get a qualified understanding of what each required would take thousands of years; which is obviously not possible.

If we could create a shortcut by familiarizing the senses with 40,000 occupations it need not take thousands of years. With an efficient sense's qualification method and computer technology perhaps much headway could be accomplished in days or even hours.

Senses and Human Activity

Can we fool the senses with some simple razzle dazzle into giving us an honest reaction to occupations? Maybe we can. Henry said "a simple answer." Our problem is that the senses are unfamiliar with 40,000 occupations. What else do we have to work with? Job tasks, human activities and actions. Let me think. Human activities? Senses are very human. The senses can pass judgment or respond to a short and concise human activity story more easily than complicated job tasks made up of several human activities and many actions. The body is familiar with the activities it does all day long. Although there are thousands of human activities, one human activity may be used in many occupations. That would appear to cut down the number of different human activities.

Senses are more familiar with and therefore have a much better chance of judging common functions (human activities and actions) than total job tasks or occupations. The senses should automatically be able to qualify an occupation where human activities and actions are familiar.

"Hold on son, what's with this razzle dazzle?" Henry injected.

"You're still here? I think I'm onto something that will work."

"Okay, assume your razzle dazzle works, and you get a more honest reaction to occupations through using senses to qualify human activities and actions. What about it? How does it help you match that dumb word maxtalability (maximum talent capability) with the right occupation?"

"It's not dumb."

"Never mind son. I like maxtals better. Let's see if I have it. You find maximum talent capability through human activities and actions that the senses have passed reasonably honest judgment on. If you find an individual's maxtalability how can you match it up with one or more of the 40,000 occupations that it fits best? You have to compare them somehow. Occupations and maximum talent capabilities are like dividing apples into oranges, they're different, not divisible."

"You're ahead of me. Let me think. Evidently all I need is a common denominator, apples into apples."

"Sure?" Henry challenged.

"Hey, I got us this far."

"Show me some more razzle dazzle."

"Okay. Okay. I think I'm on to it. Now let's see . . . common denominator? Maximum talent capabilities consist of efficient human activities. Occupations are expressed as job tasks, human activities and actions. We have occupations made up of job tasks, job tasks made up of human activities that are made up of human actions. The best common denominator for an occupation is one that is divisible into its parts, job tasks, human activities and actions. Is that okay?"

"Sounds good. Keep going," encouraged Henry.

"The common denominator isn't job tasks, because job tasks are once removed from actions, and it isn't actions, because actions are once removed from job tasks. But human activity is in the middle and touches directly on both and is divisible by both. I'm back to human activities again. Occupations and maximum talent capabilities can both be described in terms of human activities. That's it, human activity is the only logical common dominator."

"Hold on son. That is a little too fast."

"Look Henry. We already have the human activity visual library idea, them's apples. We reduce all occupations to human activities, them's apples. Human activity is the common denominator," I patiently explained.

"Wait a minute. I think you skipped something. You have a computerized visual library of 40,000 human activities and all occupations are reduced to human activities and suddenly you're home free? I don't see it. How do you use your human activity common denominator to pass an individual's maximum talent capabilities across the 40,000 occupations to find the best occupation?"

"It's simple. The Department of Labor has already catalogued and coded 20,000 occupations, which will be expanded to 40,000 occupations or more to accommodate the greater depth of occupations. We create an individual computerized human activity profile of every occupation. All these profiles are stored in an occupation profile bank in a computer. Each occupation profile consists of the code numbers of the human activities used in the occupation according to the percentage each is used. We also create a computerized human activity profile of each individual from their qualified maximum talent capability and run it across the profiles in the bank of 40,000 occupations."

"Profile?"

"Sure. Picture an artist's scissors cutting a black paper head profile of an individual at a fair. The facial features the artist cuts out have to be sharp enough so you can recognize the person, or the profile is worthless. Let's say the artist has profiles of 40,000 people in his studio. If the artist had a reason to he could take this last cutout and hold it up to each one of the 40,000 he already had, to find the best match.

"This is what we are trying to do. Human activities reduced to line bar code numbers are the facial features of the individual and occupational profiles. A similar process is used to identify fingerprints."

"Hold on, that I can visualize, but you're a little fast on this individual profile thing."

"Okay. Let's take Margo's example of a chemical oceanographer occupation. The 1986 Department of Labor's *Occupational Outlook Handbook* lists chemical oceanographer as one of eight sub-occupations under geologists and geophysicists (Department of Labor, *Dictionary Of Occupations*) as D.O.T. code number 024.161.

"These eight sub-occupations in the listed 20,000 occupations do not have code numbers; this is why the 20,000 listed occupations have been raised to a guesstimate of 40,000 occupations. Although they do not have code numbers the eight sub-occupations are distinct and separate geology occupations. They are: physical oceanographer, chemical oceanographer, hydrologist, mineralogist, paleontologist, seismologist, stratigrapher and geological oceanographer.

"All eight involve their own set of job tasks that are broken down into human activities. Each activity involves using different methods, vehicles, equipment and measuring devices. One activity would use an ocean water craft, submersible or aircraft; another would be involved on the ocean floor or ocean water strata, underground, above ground; and others in the atmosphere or mesosphere.

All use different sensing, measuring and viewing devices. Each would have a different job task and human activity profile."

"Whose fault is it if the eight occupations are not coded?"

"The lack of coding of all estimated 40,000 occupations is not a fault of The Department of Labor. Their purpose was the simplification of occupations. Ours is to interpret occupations according to human activities. The purposes are different."

"That I can understand. Which occupation is the weather man?"

"None of the above. That is a separate occupation. Meteorologist is D.O.T code no. 025 062 010. Incidentally, the meteorologist heading also has four sub-occupations without code numbers: operational or synoptic meteorologists who make weather forecasts; physical meteorologists, who do research in the atmosphere, chemical and physical properties and other weather phenomena; and finally, climatologists involved in past weather records, designing building cooling and heating systems and building better weather forecasting equipment."

"Okay, enough. I get the idea. That makes eight plus four equals twelve un-coded occupations under two coded occupation headings in the Department of Labor's list of occupations or an average of six each not coded. The current coded occupations on the Department of Labor list of 20,000 multiplied by an average of six un-coded equals 120,000 occupations to be coded. Ah! I see the problem. Instead of trying to find an individual's best occupation in 40,000 occupations it could be more like 120,000. That's why you are treading so carefully on that 40,000 figure."

"Henry, I am very hesitant to throw those kind of figures around at this time. We won't know until the coding is done."

"Okay, but where does the profile come in?"

"I'll get there," I said. "Let's stick with the work of a chemical oceanographer that is the study of the chemical composition, dissolved elements and nutrients of oceans. It could involve providing technical data important to areas such as water itself, rain, pollution, mining, construction, marine life and general research. There could be five major job tasks that occupy a chemical oceanographer's working time. Let's set up a fictitious example of the chemical oceanographer's activity time.

The Chemical Oceanographer's Activity Time

40% of the time is taking water samples. This could include above water snorkeling or diving, using sound, sensing, measuring and computer equipment.

40% of the time analyzing the samples in the lab, using microscopic and other measuring equipment.

10% of the time compiling, summarizing and recording the information onto computers.

7% of the time in the office studying maps of the area where samples are to be taken and creating a computer map of where the samples were taken.

3% of the time may be required to report results to other people and perhaps make recommendations.

There we have 100% of the time devoted to five job tasks, each of these job tasks will have a job task code number.

"Hey son, hold it. If each of the 120,000 occupations has an average of five job tasks, that makes 600,000 job tasks."

"There may be repeat job tasks that exist in many occupations," I cautioned, "such as analyzing samples in a lab. We don't know until they are coded."

"I thought we were talking about human activities. Why are we on job task codes?" Henry questioned.

"I am trying to create an understandable example using codes. I can't use coded human activities because the Dept. of Labor D.O.T. code system that indicates job tasks is not presently reduced to human activities. Stay with me."

"So the main job tasks of a chemical oceanographer's are collecting water samples and analyzing samples in the lab; with the other three tasks completing the profile. What if the oceanographer only does the lab work?"

"Then it is a different occupation. An occupation that does not entail taking water samples (40% of the chemical oceanographer's work) could be referred to as a chemical oceanographer lab technician; and of course it would have a different D.O.T. number."

"I can see each one of those would have a different job task profile but where does your human activity come in?"

"I'll show you. Back to our example. We now attempt to reduce one of the chemical oceanographer's job tasks to human activities. For instance, "taking water samples" could entail the following human activities:

"Taking water samples" Reduced to Human Activities

1. Office time spent organizing the project and determining the area where sediment samples are to be taken.
2. An on-site study of the sample area may have to be done by using the following:
   a. Swimming
   b. Snorkeling-using diving gear
   c. Using water vehicle
      1. submersible
      2. small engine aircraft with sound equipment
      3. boat
   d. Radar equipment
      1. sounding or other
      2. sensing equipment
3. Working in water:
   a. shallow ocean water
   b. deep ocean water
   c. wetlands
   d. lakes
   e. Rivers-adjacent to oceans

3. Sample-taking equipment must be transported to and from the site.
4. The equipment must be checked and kept operational.
5. The samples are:
   a. taken
   b. labeled.
6. Sample areas have to be map recorded on site.

"The chemical oceanographer's job task of collecting water samples can be reduced to at least seven distinct human activities, most of which are also influenced by sub-activities involving methods, equipment and location."

"Why do you have to break it down in such detail?"

"Each of these human activities must be coded, since these activities are subject to our senses. If you get seasick, don't like to swim, get claustrophobic in submersibles, get airsick in small engine planes or are not good mechanically your senses are going to react negatively to some of these activities. The same happens if you get bored by taking samples day after day."

"Yes I see. These are the conditions the senses dislike or cannot easily put up with. That is where the qualification factors for activity efficiency come in. Unless a person's senses like all of these activities with some consistency, it will affect their human activity efficiency in that occupation. I'm getting the picture. That's pretty neat, but does the chemical oceanographer have to do all those activities personally? Can't he or she get someone to help?"

"Depends on their job and the budget. In situations where help is allowed the workers still have to be supervised. Even then, the oceanographer may have to assist, correct or replace the helper."

"Makes sense, and those seven-plus activities are in just one of the five job tasks. By reducing all of the job tasks to human activities you have an occupational profile of a chemical oceanographer. Hey, multiply seven-plus human activities by 600,000 job tasks . . . equals?"

"Hold on, don't multiply yet. As an example, flying in small engine aircraft can be used in many job tasks across the spectrum of occupations."

"Do all occupations have as many job tasks and activities?"

"This one was quite complicated."

"Why did you choose this one. I never heard of it."

"You're right. If this was Margo's maxtalability how could she have known . . . if she never heard of it? Not many schools teach oceanography. If she saw it in a career book of some 40,000 occupations, would her brain shout out 'There's your talent?' It does not work that way. There are too many things in job tasks and activities that need to come together before people know if they are compatible with the task or not."

"There can't be too many people involved in that occupation, can there?"

"The 1992 U.S. Department of Labor *Occupational Outlook Handbook* lists over 50,000 geologists and geophysicists in the United States alone. Of these, 9,000 hold faculty positions in colleges and universities and the federal government employs 8,000. Additionally, in recent years the geology and geophysicists categories alone have added these sub-occupations to their previous listing of eight sub-occupations: aeronautical, planetary, radar, rockets, satellites and waste geologists. People are going to have a more and more difficult time exploring the occupation arena with so many new occupations coming on line."

"And all the more reason to have a talent or occupation discovery method," added Henry.

"So here we have it. We can qualify human activity with the senses. Human activity is the common denominator to run an individual's profile across the occupational profile bank to find maxtalabilities."

"Yeah, like, I think the kid's gawtit."

"Awful english, Henry," I chided. "We still have to work out the mechanics."

"No problem, that's known computer technology. There are computer specialists who can do that. The computer programmer has to convert data to detailed logical flow charts for coding into computer language. Coding is automatic. You have all the ingredients to work it. There are no unknowns that I can see. It is just a case of compiling the data. You know, son, you get way ahead of me at times."

"I know, our employees used to say that about me. I hate details; I like ideas and solutions. I jump right to the end. Incidentally, coming from you, that was quite wordy."

"So I got carried away. Wait a minute. You may have forgotten something you can't jump over. The senses qualification, common denominator process and occupation profile are all workable; but you're not into the genes or the brain to find an individual's efficient human activities to create the individual maxtalability profile with your razzle dazzle."

"We'll do it."

"Show me." Blip.

"Henry? . . . Henry?" He's gone again. He's right. We are still not into the brain to qualify talents. Ah, but we have a common denominator, senses that can qualify; and that computer profile idea is awesome. Now we have a method to bridge the gap between occupations and an individual's maxtalability profile.

There is another advantage to human activities. Occupations and job tasks may not be familiar to people in other areas of the world, but human activities are common human actions and they will be much more language interpretable.

There may be a new problem. Will the individual profile be clear cut or sharp enough to run across the occupational profile bank to select the best maxtalabilities? The individual maxtalability profile must be sharp enough to be recognized by the occupation profiles in the occupation profile bank.

We also need to bypass the influence of occupational misconceptions to allow an individual free and clear appraisal of an occupation's job tasks and activities. Is there a shorter method to penetrate or communicate with genes or the brain to find an individual's maxtalabilities to create their profiles? We may have been lucky thus far. The remaining problems are very perplexing. How can there be a simple answer? Research of genetics and the mind did not provide a clue to brain penetration. This one really scares me. What do I do or where do I go to find an answer? Perhaps there isn't an answer.

16

Penetrating the Brain
August 1993

*An uninformed interest is merely a reaction to the
thing which arouses liking or disliking. An
intelligent interest is one where the activity
has been subdivided into its component parts and
the person knows that he likes several parts,
dislikes possibly certain other parts, and is
indifferent to the rest.*

EDWARD K. STRONG JR.,
VOCATIONAL INTERESTS OF MEN AND WOMEN

Scientists are researching the human mind, the most capable problem solver in the world, and they are on the brink of understanding how the brain works; but we know nothing of talent.

Scientists have penetrated genes and are now able to correct gene dysfunction, but talent genes, if they exist, are unknown. I am forced to find some other way to penetrate the brain to develop a talent discovery method. This has been the most difficult problem from the beginning. All of my previous work will have been in vain if we cannot solve it. I have tried every angle, researched the brain and genetics, and still there is nothing. After coming this far I may have failed. Nothing has come to me for months.

Alaska-August 1993

On our fall vacation we sailed aboard the Westerdam to Juneau, Alaska. From there we traveled westward by bus to Dawson City, Yukon Territory, Canada where we boarded the M.V. Yukon Queen for a hundred mile journey north on the Yukon River. I mention this trip because while sitting outside in the back of the river launch, with a gentle breeze blowing in my face, another fleeting thought crossed my mind. It just touched me, and then disappeared. I could not bring it back; the same as with the string of pearls in Vancouver. I don't know what happened this time, maybe I was distracted by the view.

We disembarked on a rocky shore at Eagle, Alaska where we picked up our motor coach to take us to Tok, Alaska. On the way to Tok we stopped at a village named Chicken. Chicken? Why would anyone want to name a village Chicken? The story was: two early miners had a plentiful supply of ptarmigan to hunt in the area so they decided to name the village Ptarmigan. The problem was they could not find anyone who could spell Ptarmigan, so they named this little outpost Chicken until someone could tell them how to spell Ptarmigan; evidently no one ever did.

Back on the bus on our way to Tok I took a short nap. When I awoke, there it was. "I think I have it. I know how to get into the brain," I said to Donna, who was seated next to me.

"Please, not mine dear," she replied matter-of-factly.

"No, I mean to find a person's talent. You know, what I've been looking for all this time."

"Yes dear, I know . . . that's nice."

"You don't get very excited when I come up with valuable solutions."

"Well dear husband, I expect it. You're always coming up with something when we are on a trip. Every time you have a problem or need a solution we may have to take a trip."

The lady is smart too.

The fleeting glimpse was in reference to the "Getting to Know You" exercise I developed years ago to be used after an individual's Strong test indicated certain occupations. How does this connect with brain penetration?

The occupational and interest tests such as Strong, are comparative tests used to locate career interests; but tests cannot tell us what we are or what we can do best. Test results are based on interests not human activities. Could interests be an entry into the brain? Is that possible or am I grasping at straws? I think I need help with this.

"Tests and interests won't get you into the brain."

"Henry, what are you doing up here in Alaska?"

"Where you go, I go."

"Oh? Well all right. Henry! Can we get into the brain through interests in some way? Some interests are discoverable and can be worked with."

"Interests are not trustworthy. Remember the problem of misinterpretations and misconceptions?" Henry reminded.

"Yes I know, but it's all I have. How about this? The brain can picture itself doing a simple activity. Generally it knows human activities it can do best, is capable of doing or prefers."

"You already have the occupation human activity profile bank idea and those are apples. You can't get into the brain with occupational interests, those are lemons . . . not compatible. You cannot create an interest profile and run it across the human activity occupation bank to find maxtalabilities."

"When an individual takes a career or interest test the results show a number of occupational interests. Those interest occupations can be reduced to job tasks and then human activities." I stopped. "There it is. That's the key. I think I've got it. That's where the 'Getting to know you' fleeting glimpse comes in."

"How is that?"

"Every individual has knowledge of a few occupations. We reduce those occupations and occupations from their interest tests to human activities. The like human activities go onto a human activity list. The most often repeated human activities will be placed at the top of the list to set a trend for starting an individual's profile.

"Hold on son I'm a little slow. What human activity list are we talking about?"

"An individual makes a list of preferred occupations or job tasks based upon past experience, tests, other knowledge and exposure. These preferred occupations and job tasks are reduced to a list of human activities, which are then reviewed by the individual in our human activity visual library. The like human activities that survive (pass) the viewing process go up on a human activity list with those human activities appearing most often at the top of the list and on down. By having the individual review the visuals of all these occupations, we build a like list of human activities for the individual from that we can build an individual profile ; the individual's mind does the work for us."

"Oh?"

"You don't sound convinced. It was the 'Getting to Know You' exercise I had Margo and other people do at the library. By looking up the best occupations on her Strong test, I had her make a page of the likes, indifference and dislikes of the job tasks for each of those occupations, including the occupations above and below each occupation listing. Then transferring the likes and dislikes from all the pages to a master list with those most often repeated at the top."

"I remember. But 'Getting to Know You' is a job task exercise list, not a human activity list," challenged Henry.

"Exactly. We are using the job task idea but carrying it one step further by reducing job tasks to human activities and using a computer instead of doing it manually."

"But what makes you think you are getting good human activity imput from occupations we already agreed are flawed by lack of knowledge and misconceptions?"

"It does not make any difference, we only need an entry way of some preferred activities to get into the brain."

"Well okay, go on," he conceded. "I want to hear the rest."

"From the individual's human activity list we create a human activity computer profile of the individual. Remember apples and apples. Then we run the individual profile across the occupation library bank and come up with new occupations that best match the individual's profile. We could call this the first stage profile. Here's where winnowing comes in. We reduce the new occupations to human activities, the individual visually reviews them and we add any new like or preferred human activities to the individual's previous human activity list. The effect of the addition of the new activities automatically adjusts the list to accommodate the increasing number of those activities that appear on the list. This changes the list and results in a new or adjusted second stage profile of the individual. This profile is more definitive because we have added more preferred human activities and increased the repeats.

"Running this new profile across the occupation bank, the computer throws out more occupations and the process is repeated again and again, refining the profile more and more. When no new occupations come up, and the occupations continue to repeat, we are in a preliminary maxtalability area," I explained.

"I understand that but you jumped into that human activity list awfully fast. How do you know you're getting good human activity input or enough applicable starting occupations reduced to activities to have repeats to create a sharp image? If you don't get enough repeats you won't have a profile the computer can work with."

"It has to happen, every individual identifies some occupations in the Strong test and from them we reduce them to human activities. Each individual has a human activity preference personality that will retouch certain human activities in different occupations. Through those most often repeated human activities we have an opening to use a winnowing process. Each time we winnow a new profile, the profile image becomes sharper and sharper until it can make efficient occupation match-ups.

"Let's start with seven interesting occupations. Each occupation may have an average of five job tasks and the average job task may have an average of five human activities. This equals 175 human activities from seven occupations. 7 x 5=35 x 5 = 175. Let's say one third or fifty-seven of the human activities are likes and five likes are repeated twice, equaling fifty-two different like human activities on the list with the top five occurring twice. From this we create an original profile.

"Now we run or winnow the individual profile across the occupation profile library bank and from the matched occupations the computer throws out the individual selects seven (arbitrary figure) more occupations. Now we have another 175 like, indifference and dislikes; and at least another 57 preferred activities; and instead of only five activities at the top of the list that are repeated twice, we may now have activities that appear three or four times. Each time we winnow we add to the activities at the top of the list. We are naturally going to have more likes from the new occupations because the profile is becoming sharper."

"What if the same occupations come up?" challenged Henry.

"Eventually we want them to; but in the beginning it is not very likely, not with 40,000 occupations and who knows how many human activities? In the end, when the same occupations keep coming up they are maxtalabilities. The winnowing process has done its original job."

"Very good," said Henry. "I can see how it will work. The selection process is as old as the IBM card sort system. It will certainly work. To what degree of efficiency it will work for each individual we won't know until it is done.

Here's a question. Why go though all that converting when you could do the same by scrolling through the human activity visual library and placing all the preferred's on the list?"

"Scrolling through a human activity library will only bring up each activity once. We need repeats. We need the benefit of the individual's human activity preference personality exerting itself more with each winnowing step. The first profile may not be a sufficient exercise to give us valid occupations but if we continue to winnow it down further and further, it will come closer to maxtalabilities."

"Anything else we can do to assure repeats?"

"The computer programmers who set up the profiles may design their own or better efficient ways of creating repeats, including job task profiles and adding dislikes to the profile. It is up to the computer programmers to design the most efficient system."

Henry was a great help by asking the right questions, but he was not through yet.

17

Matching People With Occupations

*Finding yourself represents the first, or
identifying, stage of what we shall refer to as the
identity-match process. Once you have found
yourself, the matching half of this process involves
capability matching your personality and talent
traits with broadly defined job functions for which
these traits are desirable.*

CHARLES GUY MOORE, THE CAREER GAME

H enry wanted to know how the chemical oceanographer
profile would be set-up. "Give me an example of how you
are going to make a profile match between the human
activity repeat list profile and the chemical oceanographer profile, "
he requested.

"Good question," I said. "Let's go back to the chemical oceanographer occupation and create a job task profile."

"Why job tasks? I'm already convinced that human activities are
the common denominator. You're confusing me again," complained
Henry. "We were working with seven human activities."

"Stay with me, Henry," I urged. "For this example it will be
easier to understand using five job tasks. Using seven activities plus

a-b-c sub-activities may not be complicated for a computer but could be very complicated for a lay person to understand."

"I like your non-tech approach," said Henry.

Job Task Time use Breakdown of a Chemical Oceanographer

40%	Takes samples-could include above water, swimming and diving.
40%	Analyzes the samples in the lab, using microscopic and other measuring equipment.
10%	Compiles and summarizes the information.
7%	Makes maps of the area where samples are taken.
3%	Records and recommends.
100%	of the time is involved in the five job tasks.

"Back to our job task example. Let's give each one of the job tasks a fictitious code number."

"What factors are used to make up a code number?" Henry questions.

"The code number could, as an example, identify with the worker functions already determined by the Department Of Labor, the list I previously referred to. Some of the functions found in a chemical oceanographer occupation could be: analyzing, coordinating, innovating, compiling-computing, comparing, supervising, taking instruction, setting-up, precision working, operating-controlling, manipulating, and speaking-signaling. We could also add the 'where,' the ocean and lab; and the 'what,' water chemistry. The 'who' would be solo with some supervision and team work. When combined, we may need these additional factors for a more definitive profile, and all of these factors may be worked into a job task code."

"I get the idea," responded Henry. "This is computer programmer area again."

"I agree. Let's get back to our example. The following is a way of matching using job tasks. We repeat the previous fictitious example of an oceanographer job task breakdown and compare it to an occupation thrown out by Margo's profile in the winnowing process, but now we are adding fictitious job task code numbers.

Chemical Oceanographer Time Use by Job Task Code Numbers

40%   Job task code no. S 241 086-42
40%   Job task code no. R 034 462-3
10%   Job task code no. A 911 220-74
 7%   Job task code no. S 642 321-86
 3%   Job task code no. C 121 071-27

Now let's say Margo had the following (top five repeats) on her job task list:

1.	15 repeats =	42%	Job task code no. R 034 462-3
2.	12 repeats =	33%	Job task code no. S 241 086-42
3.	4 repeats =	11%	Job task code no. A 911 220-74
4.	3 repeats =	8%	Job task code no. C 121 071-23
5.	2 repeats =	6%	Job task code no. S 642 321-86
	36 repeats =	100%	of the top five job tasks.

"The first job task of the chemical oceanographer's job task time use is code number S 241 086-42 and was repeated on Margo's list 12 times or 33% of the time. The second job task, code number R 034 462-3, was repeated on Margo's list 15 times or 42% of the time. The third job task, code number A 911 220-74, was repeated four times or 11% of the time. The fourth job task, code number S 642 321-86 was repeated twice or 6% of the time. The fifth job task, code number C 121 071-27, was not a match."

"Where did that new underlined code number C 121 071-23 come from? It's on Margo's profile but not on the oceanographer profile."

"It could be a single (no repeat) on Margo's job task list or not on her list at all. It may be a dislike or she may never have been exposed to it to pass judgment on."

"I see, but the profile didn't work, its not a perfect match"

"There never will be a perfect match. As an example subtracting 8% for the number four (no show) job task on Margo's list still leaves us with a 92% efficient match; which may be our maximum winnowing effort. Again, this interpretation method is up to the programmers."

"Are all Margo's likes on her profile, even the singles?" queried Henry.

"They could be; if the programmers can use them. Because Margo had no C 121 071-27 on her job task list it may have been on her list once or not at all. The whole list becomes a backup for those most often repeated."

"I see it now. That's where maxtalability comes in. You're getting the maximum occupation match the job task profile can provide when comparing Margo's profile with the 40,000 occupations."

"You got it," I said.

"And if you had another occupation at a 90% match and another at 88% match those would be quite close to maxtalabilities and worth looking into."

"Right."

"Could job task code No. C 121 071-27, on the oceanographer profile but not on Margo's profile, be a dislike for her, and still find oceanographer an acceptable match?"

"It could, if the first four job tasks are weighted heavily enough to diminish the effect. The occupation may be able to exclude or replace that job task or the dislike may lose its negative personality when attached to the rest of the positive activities," I replied.

"How could that happen?"

"The dislike job task may be in a more acceptable environment in that occupation or be more important or contributory thus changing the character of the dislike to indifference or like."

"What if a person sees a job task repeated? What is to stop them from saying to themselves 'this was just added to the job task list and I don't have to judge or add it again?' "

"They can't," I replied. "If a job task is from a new occupation, the computer will not continue until they enter a decision. They have to make a judgment on every job task. That is how we get our repeats."

"Right."

"Let's get back to human activities," I suggest. We have just seen how a grouping of Margo's job task profile best matches a chemical oceanographer job task profile."

"Yes, I see. She should be great in that field. What if a certain human activity is rare and another one common? The common one would have a better chance to repeat on her activity list."

"Once the original winnowing process is completed the individual should review a list of allied activities. Let's say the individual scrolls through the unrepeated "like" activities and finds that one is very interesting. The individual could temporarily insert this activity in any position they choose on his/her activity list and run that profile. This would no doubt bring up new occupations. That gives an individual even more choices for their repeat lists. There will be other kinds of activity profile solitaire a person can play once the original winnowing is completed to come up with additional new occupations.

"The programmers may find it important to give an importance weight to occupations according to how often a human activity is repeated in the 40,000 occupations. When the cataloguing and coding is done the programmers will know how often each human activity occurs."

"The winnowing is then even more versatile," commented Henry.

"That's right," I agreed. "And remember we aren't doing this, the individual's mind is doing it. We are into the brain."

"By George, sounds like you have it, but wait. Who will pay for the work of reducing 40,000 occupations to human activities, creating the visual library of human activities and the profiles? Will individuals, businesses, government or education shell out millions of dollars on an unproved theory? You can't winnow one individual profile until the 40,000 occupations are profiled."

"I know this is a problem," I conceded. "We can only hope there will be enough influential people who will take a strong interest in this concept and demand that the work be done. At first, only a few people might agree with my arguments, but from a few the movement for talent discovery can build quickly.

"Let's hope your right that there are people out there who understand and care enough" Blip.

I am completely amazed at this step forward in penetrating the brain. It is unbelievable that it could be found! The penetration works and solves so many problems. It is both incredible and wonderful . . . and so simple.

In the future there may be other ways into the brain. For now we have only one way in which to fool the brain into sharing its knowledge . . . through interests that identify occupations, reduced to job tasks, then to human activities. We are so close, only one step away from a method of discovering an individual's maximum talents.

We still have the problem of how to bypass the distortion caused by misconceptions the brain and the senses have accumulated. Also we have to assure that we have adequate sources of preferred interests in certain occupations to make the human activity list effective. If both of these things be done, are there any more problems?

18

Interest Sources Converted

*...there is little doubt that a consideration of
interests can make a substantial contribution to
answering the challenge of locating people in the
kind of work they will enjoy.*

FREDERICK KUDER,
ACTIVITY INTERESTS AND OCCUPATIONAL CHOICE

Our search for a method to identify an individual's maximum talents has led us to interests converted to occupations that are then converted to human activities. We have established that a human activity repeat list is the vehicle through which we can make use of the brain's knowledge without actually penetrating the brain.

What is an interest? The following quote does not tell us what interest is; but it may give us an indication of how interest works:

*It is difficult to avoid the almost incredible
conclusion that everything is submitted to the
cortex for recognition and preliminary assessment
at the unconscious level - on the strength the
arousal system damps down both sense organs and
channels, as well as analyzing equipment, for those*

that of which are of lessor interest and boosts those
which are needed for more interesting data.
GORDON RATTRAY TAYLOR, THE NATURAL HISTORY OF THE MIND

We do not know if interest originates in the cortex of the brain, only that at times the brain seems to be involved in interest judgment. Scientific research is just starting to investigate what interests are, where they originate and how human interests perform. Without scientific background it is difficult to follow the path of interests that lead us into the maze of the brain where the knowledge of talent capability must exist; so again, I must proceed on my own.

Without interest life cannot endure. We know nothing about human interest; strange. Without an interest in something or someone people fade into non-existence.

Interests are as necessary as breath; their absence can terminate breath for lack of a reason to live. Interests are the essence and vitality of our lives. Interests are a most valuable trait of all humans. Being that important, is there an area of the brain that has as its purpose the sponsorship of interests leading to talents?

Observing Interests

What are the indications that interest has been stimulated? Is it arousal, attention, awareness . . . all of which are sponsored by the need to experience pleasure or avoid displeasure? Are there two kinds of interest: that which appeals to our physical appetite and that which appeals to our intellect? Additionally, interests would have to be divided between activities an individual is capable of performing and those activities which they are not capable of. How would this distinction be accomplished?

After years of testing and interviewing disinterested people with dull expressions, non-caring attitudes and stoops in their posture, I have often seen the person's eyes suddenly light up when something particular (of interest) was said. In these circumstances people would sit up straighter and pay attention more closely. However, as soon as the subject was changed, they would fade again.

When I see eyes light up I know something of value is going on behind those eyes. Was a delight nerve touched? Did a neuronic impulse flash across a pleasant feeling area? Interest or the ability to originate interest is obviously a natural human trait; there seems to be something that will light every individual's eyes.

There seems to be no relationship between what lights up eyes and what people are capable of doing; yet there must be some positive value to that reaction. Is it an indication of interest that may lead to a source of talent capability? Can we get into that neuron maze of the brain and find out what a certain interest means?

When Isaac Newton's eyes lit up it was called genius. When Einstein's eyes lit up it was called genius. Although having one's eyes light up is not necessarily an indication of genius or even a completed idea or invention, perhaps it is only an indication of an interest to do so. One thing we have in common with geniuses is that a particular subject can light up our eyes too. My experience indicates that every person has an interest that can light up their eyes.

In areas where physical capabilities are important, physical talent itself may sponsor interest as the individual becomes involved with sports, music or art. However an interest in one of these areas can dominate an individual's life and may deter the individual from seeking a less obvious and more valuable talent.

An individual's store room of interests, carefully filtered, may provide clues to areas of interest or capability. It bothered me that the brain cannot automatically pre-qualify activities that are not good for a person or that the person cannot do well. We know so little of where interests originate or how they operate.

A person who has talent in one occupation such as music, will probably find it difficult to apply that talent to a different activity, such as biology, and achieve equal efficiency. This may be partially true because a violinist may not have an equal interest in biology. Interest can influence human activity.

Interests can change with the environment. An interest in a particular occupation may be unacceptable in one business environment while acceptable in a different business environment. A receptionist in an advertising agency may not be happy as a receptionist in a salt packaging factory.

What is Interest?

An interest is an activity that sparks our attention and lights up our eyes. It is an activity we have a desire to witness, work with, participate in or enjoy. An interest can be work, a hobby or entertainment we either observe or participate in.

Webster defines interest:

noun: readiness to be concerned with or moved by

syn: concern, curiosity, regard

rel: enthusiasm, excitement, passion, attention, care, concernment, absorption, engrossment.

verb: to engage the attention and interest of

syn: appeal, attract, excite, fascinate, intrigue

rel: arouse, tantalize, titillate, lure, pull, snare, tempt.

As we can see, interests are the story of life.

Everyone Has Different Interests

We are not all interested or turned on by the same things; it is part of our personality that makes us different and unique. The scope of interests includes sex, a biological necessity for mankind's survival, and every activity to the end of life.

There are many different levels of interest. Every individual has the same genetic structure but each genetic personality sponsors or originates their own special set of interests. Each individual has a specific and distinct interest personality, as divergent as our fingerprints or facial features.

We do not know how interests originate or where they come from. Do we inherit them genetically or are they aroused by instinct? Do they come from experience, the environment or do they originate from our individual genetic personality? Interests are so key to our lives that the ability to have interests must be a genetic creation.

Are interests inspired by challenge or some pleasantness we feel? Are interests more related to certain activities than to occupations or job tasks? Interest is a mystery we cannot solve at this time. Perhaps talent discovery will stimulate science to further research interest, for interest could be a key to human talent.

Does every person have an interest in something? What is the difference between an interest and the activity an interest may refer to? Does every interest have a corresponding mental or physical activity? Can occupations be reduced to interests rather than activities? An activity is either interesting to a person or it is not. Would there be value to cataloguing interests?

We are penetrating the brain through interest tests that identify occupations and reducing occupations to human activities. It is the only way we have at present to penetrate the brain.

For our purpose we may have to approach the subject of interest from a practical viewpoint rather than as a genetic/biological function of the brain. To penetrate the brain we need to jar the mind with as many sources of interests we can develop.

+ Interest sources from the individual from work or activities experienced firsthand.
+ Knowledge of occupations that an individual has seen (TV, movies), heard of or read about.
+ Work or activities that an individual has hearsay of or second-hand exposure from family and friends.

+ School activities.
+ Occupations suggested from interest or career tests. (I have never seen a Strong test that did not highlight some occupations.)
+ Occupations or activities an individual may dream about.
+ Analyzing an individual's known skills.

Interest Source Stimulation

To refresh their memories, an individual could use a computer to scroll through a visual list of occupations they have prior knowledge of; there are hundreds of such visuals now available and more being developed.

Scrolling through a job task visual library may locate interests.

Scrolling through a human activity visual library may emphasize certain interests.

Our obvious objective is to uncover interests in an individual's brain, convert these interests to occupations and then back down to human activities. We have established sources of interests, though there may be more; and we are making use of brain-sponsored interests to penetrate the brain. It may not be the best answer but we are into the brain.

We have one last problem: the brain and senses are subject to distortion caused by misconceptions. Nothing seems to be coming from our normal sources or from the subconscious. Let it grind for awhile. Maybe it will start pushing again when it is ready.

19

Intelligence and Creativity
January 1995

*Creativity is not a mystical talent that some people
have and others can only envy. Lateral thinking is
the type of creative thinking that can be learned,
practiced and used by everyone . . . Lateral
thinking will not make everyone a genius but it
will supplement existing thinking skills with a
valuable ability to generate new ideas.*
EDWARD DE BONO, *SERIOUS CREATIVITY*

This winter I am making no headway in misconceptions, so I will go back to writing novels. It is great fun and perhaps my subconscious will try to make a helpful point in the story.

Not on our Planet, a new story, emerges in my mind; it is about a young, male sociologist from earth who meets a young, female biologist from a sister planet in orbit on the other side of the sun. Although both planets are equal in development, her planet does not have our earthly problems of crime, drugs, disease, poverty, pollution, population control and war. Their educational system developed talent discovery generations ago; thereby unleashing the talent of their people that contained and prevents these major problems.

There it is, the sneaky subconscious interfering again, clarifying talent discovery.

Her planet is deathly afraid of earth, they know it is only a matter of time before earthlings find and contaminate them with earth's "external" culture. Their "internal" culture does not over value external appearances rather it highly values the internal self (what a person thinks about themselves). Personal integrity, truth and ethics in dealing with others are of prime concern. Everyone is recognized as equally intelligent and uses their talents for the benefit of all.

Her planet offers to show us how to find and use our talents, so we may also contain our problems. Great story. I love it. I hope to complete it someday.

The key to the story is obviously finding and using the talents of our people to prevent and contain our problems. By comparing the two planets my subconscious has impressed upon me the imperative need and value of talent discovery, and this makes me very uncomfortable. We have to develop talent discovery as soon as possible.

Leaving the story behind, my mind is now back to reality and my search for talent discovery. The word 'intelligence' starts to cause me concern again. Where did I last hear the word intelligence? Of course, in the Not On Our Planet story. On that planet everyone is recognized as equally intelligent and uses their talents for the benefit of all. Interesting, but I don't see how that fits in.

It does however raise an important question. Although everyone here on earth has maxtalabilities, can we establish that everyone has the intelligence to use individual maxtalabilities if found? This is obviously very important for Talent Discovery would be little use to those who may not have the intelligence to make use of their talents. I don't need one more problem, but I can't ignore it. I will need help with this touchy subject. "Henry? Help!"

"I figured you would get to this 'everybody having intelligence' idea sooner or later."

"Now you're anticipating me?"

"So?"

"Did you feed that intelligence concept to me in the *Not On Our Planet* story?"

"Questions. Questions. You know I don't answer questions," replies Henry. "Back to your remaining problem."

"There are two problems now: misinterpretations and people having equal or available intelligence."

"As I said, back to the one remaining intelligence problem."

Why is Henry so insistent on one remaining problem? Oh well. "I don't know where to start," I admit.

"Cm'on son. What is intelligence? You have a dictionary, don't you?"

"I think I know what intelligence is."

"Let's hear it," he challenges.

"As I remember, the difference between man and animal is man can take two things and make a useful third out of them. This is referred to as human intelligence. Intelligence is innovation, creativity, improving something or problem solving. These activities are the result of using intelligence as a mental tool. All humans can do these things; so it is logical that all humans have intelligence.

"Humans, as well as animals, have knowledge of the things they need to know," I continued. "Some animals are clever and all animals have the knowledge needed to survive; but animals do not have the intelligence to create complicated things; so just having knowledge may not be the most important part of human intelligence. The dictionary places more emphasis on using knowledge in human reasoning, understanding, problem solving and adapting knowledge to new situations. An individual may lack knowledge but that does not deny them intelligence capability."

"Very good son, so you believe that all humans have intelligence capability?"

"It seems logical and there is much to support it, but if it is true that everyone has equal intelligence capability; then why does society set intelligence standards as if to say by inference certain classes of people are more intelligent than others? Has it come about unconsciously, by design, or is it a next and timely step in human evolution whose time has come?"

"Good question," Henry encourages, "but if all people have intelligence and talent why are these qualities not more common?"

"The answer is most people do not believe they have a high level of intelligence or talent. Education sets perimeters early in life identifying children who do not meet certain memorizing standards as less intelligent than other children. This stigmatizing continues through the growing years and those identified as less intelligent ultimately accept their fate.

"The only time an individual can break out of this net is when, usually through an accident, they have an unfettered opportunity to show what they can do. They are then surprised at their ability and take off with a vengeance."

"That sounds like an acceptable explanation. Other than the few who breakout, it sounds like a tragedy of substantial magnitude for most people. Tell me, are all human brains the same size?" Henry asks.

"A human brain weighs about three pounds. There are no normal five- or one-pound brains. Oh, I see what you're getting at. All human brains are the same size; therefore appearing to have equal brain capacity?"

"How about genes?" Henry continues.

"It appears we may have established that a full complement of genes is necessary for humans to exist at all," I matter-of-factly reply.

"How about creativity?"

"Edward deBono says creativity is not a mystical talent that only some people have, it can be learned. If all people can learn to be creative and intelligence is needed to be creative, then again it seems logical all people have equal intelligence capability."

We are creative beings. Our natural instincts,
desires and tendencies are toward creating. The
desire to create is not limited by beliefs, nationality,

creed, educational background or era. This urge
resides in all of us.
ROBERT FRITZ, *THE PATH OF LEAST RESISTANCE*

"It may be safe to accept that talent applies intelligence to knowledge as a tool to enhance creativity," I continue. "The maximum use of talent capability is also expressed in creativeness. So the direction of both human intelligence and human talent is towards creativity."

"Very good," Henry says. "Let's go back to synergism and intelligence."

"Funny you should bring that up. It just occurred to me too. Okay, when considering the action that takes place in a synergistic field using a complementary group of efficient human activities the result is creativity. So the synergistic field must consist of utilizing an individual's intelligence. If you find maxtalability it may uncover the necessary intelligence.

Maxtalability provides the needed environment to efficiently apply intelligence to knowledge for creativity to grow. Hence, all people may show adequate intelligence capabilities when exposed to their maxtalabilities. Maxtalability turns on the intelligence/creative switch. How about that? That is an answer."

"Makes good sense. So what is creativity?"

"Ah, yes. Creativity is human beauty. . . a blessed creation. True creativity must be nurtured like a plant; you have to give it everything it needs and then stand back and let it grow. It can be nurtured in its natural surroundings but will grow and bloom at it's own leisure. It is like the fragrance of growing flowers that penetrate your senses without warning. It is as sensitive as a wild flower that dies in your hand when picked.

"Creativity appears like a small, white, puffy cloud floating by in a vast blue sky; it is as gentle as a breeze on a quiet and humid summer day. It appears from anywhere and nowhere. Creativity is like a puff of smoke, you run your hand through it and it is gone. Nothing is more sensitive . . . as fleeting. Human creativity is the precious advantage humans have over all other living things. It is in all of us to some degree and available in great amounts when it is in the presence of talent. Creativity is the beauty and wonder of intelligence at work."

"Hey son, you sure get flowery at times," comments Henry. "That was very nice and mighty poetic, but back to business. So all people will show intelligence when their maxtalabilities are discovered?"

"Perhaps only if they want to be creative in their talent. The choice is theirs. I can't see anyone not wanting to be," I said, "however all people are different, some may have more creative interest than others. As an example, "right brainer's" like to create new things and are more creative than "left brainer's," who like to examine and record existing things; both could have a similar talent capability but "right brainer's" may choose not to concentrate their efforts on creative ability. Creativity can be learned, although some may prefer to use their talents in other ways. Intelligence is expressed in terms of creativity, so intelligence may also be learned. It may be proved one day that all have equal intelligence capability. I don't believe God short-changed anyone."

"What about the great people of history, were they more intelligent?" posed Henry.

"The few people in history who stand out were not overly intelligent or great in more than one or two talent areas. They may have been fortunate enough to have had the opportunity and environment to use their particular talent capability but there has never been a human with talent that could be applied to every activity of life. People with a broad spectrum of imagination and inventiveness had their problems too. They were intelligent about their talent, not necessarily about their life itself. They were not perfect people.

"Like life, talent is the challenge to strive towards perfection, not perfection itself. I doubt a perfect person could or would want to exist in our imperfect world. I think the good Lord knew this;

which is why we are created as imperfect as we are. We are all cut out of the same mold: there is no evidence that any one person has or ever has had more brain capacity or intelligence than anyone else. Those who try to teach superiority principles according to gender or race have been proven wrong many times."

"Well! . . . very good and profound. Let's summarize what you said," suggests Henry. "You have established that all humans have creativity and intelligence or they can be learned. Intelligence is a necessary application, along with compatible human activities that modify the synergistic process resulting in maxtalability. All people have adequate brain capacity, the necessary genes and talent capability to make use of intelligence. So there ya are. That wasn't so hard, now was it?" Blip.

"Henry?" He's gone again. I'm sure glad that's out of the way. I guess I knew those things in a vague way; but I needed his help to bring them together. I wonder why Henry dodged the still lingering and haunting misconception problem? Will the last piece fall into place?

The last problem I need to overcome is how to bypass individuals' misconceptions. How can we penetrate the brain to do that?

At the start of each day I try to summarize in one statement the stage talent discovery is at and the problems yet to be solved. One morning I unconsciously typed this statement: "To find maxtalabilities we must take the individual out of the interest, occupation and job task arena into the area of human activities, where misinterpretations of known occupations and job tasks lose their identity and cease to be influential." I read it again. How could I have missed that all this time?

Human activities, where experience and opinions resulting in misrepresentations of known occupations and job tasks lose their identity and cease to be influential.

Let's see, misinterpretations and misconceptions are false im-

pressions of work or occupations. The brain can misinterpret occupations but is less likely to misinterpret job tasks and most unlikely
to misinterpret a single human activity comprised of everyday known
combinations of body actions and thought patterns. The mind can
picture itself doing a simple activity and is unlikely to be confused
by that activity.

The senses can respond easier to human activities that are simple
and uncomplicated stories and so pass fairly honest judgment. By
reducing occupations to human activities we have automatically
eliminated the heavy effect of misinterpreting occupations. The problem of misinterpretation is substantially reduced.

So there it is, occupations and job tasks lose misinterpretation
identity when reduced to human activities. Why was it I did not see
it before? It was right there in front of me all the time. Sometimes
when we state the problem in different ways the problem ceases to
exist. It is all so obvious. Henry did not acknowledge the problem
because he knew there was none. He knew all along. We did it.
Shouldn't bells peal or something?

"Henry, are you there? I need another opinion. Is it true the
talent discovery process is now workable or am I imagining things?"

"You're only supposed to call when you have a problem."

"Sorry . . . well . . . are there any more problems?"

"I don't know of any. So you made it, you worked your way
through to the riddle of solving one of every individual's most difficult needs. How do you feel about it?"

I'm numb. I can't believe it. As I have said before, how could
someone like me with my poor education and back ground do something as complicated as this?"

"There is a very logical reason."

"I don't know what you mean."

"Think." suggested Henry. "It would have to be someone like
you."

"Why?"

"You with your unlikely education and background are the proof of talent discovery itself. You said it:

'What any individual can dream, that individual has intelligence and capability to make the dream come true with discovered talents.'

You are the best proof of maximum talent capability by what you have accomplished. You had the belief and sustained interest to do it: your mind allowed you to keep at it: your senses approved it: you applied intelligence to a set of efficient matched abilities so that synergism was activated and creativity solved the problem."

"I'm amazed, I still can't believe it."

"Don't get carried away, Maximum Talent Capabilities time has come, if you had not done it perhaps someone else would have."

"Henry that's a logical deduction, it sounds right. But why me."

"You just accidentally had the right genes in the right place and at the right time. And then . . . perhaps it was not an accident."

"That is even more astonishing—and has many implications . . ."

"Doesn't it though?" Henry said thoughtfully. "And another observation, because of this discovery we may be on the door step of a very different and better world."

This journey started in far away Egypt and finally all of the links in the chain have come together. I am certain future generations will find new and better ways of making talent discovery more efficient. Our search for a talent discovery method has led us to maxtalability . . . the maximum talent capability that everyone possesses in some unknown area.

The Talent Discovery concept is workable; and once completed will be available for the benefit of all people.

20

The Talent Discovery Concept

*Although there is no taxonomy of talents or system
of talents classification that is widely accepted,
talent is recognized as a set of aptitudes and
abilities that predispose an individual to superior
performance or achievement.*

CONCEPTIONS OF GIFTEDNESS,
EDITED BY ROBERT STERNBERG & JANET E. DAVIDSON

Our search has been for positive talents that compliment our well-being in occupations in which we can use our talents. Through the senses we can qualify human activities. Talent is a highly efficient and qualified group of human activities that compliment each other in some specific and positive area. Efficient human activities working together are synergistically enhanced in a field of intelligence resulting in maxtalability.

Obviously a trial run of the Talent Discovery process has not been possible until the necessary software needed is completed; however, prior to actual development this is how we visualize it being done. The following is a step by step visualizing of the Talent Discovery process:

1.   Submit an individual to an interest questionnaire. The interests are converted to occupations that are reduced to job tasks and finally to preferred human activities.

2.   Submit an individual to interest tests that suggest occupations. Reduce the occupations to job tasks and finally to human activities.

3.   Each human activity is available through audiovisual and, if possible, via Virtual Reality simulation so that the individual can qualify by like, dislike or indifference his/her response to the activity.

4.   The like, preferred or qualified human activities appear on a computer human activity profile list with the most-often mentioned human activities at the top of the list and on down.

5.   When all of the human activities are viewed an individual profile is generated from the human activity list.

6.   All estimated 40,000 occupations are individually reduced to a human activity profiles and stored in a computer bank.

7.   The individual human activity profile is compared with the occupation human activity bank of profiles to find seven (as an example) new occupations that closely match the individual profile, and the computer emits a new set of occupations.

8.   The new occupations are reduced to job tasks and finally to human activities.

9.   The new human activities are viewed and the like human

activities that survive are merged with the original human activity list with the most often repeated activities appearing at the top and on down.

10. The human activity list is now changed because of the additions, and a new individual human activity profile is created. Every change in the human activity list will change the individual profile.

11. The new or second stage individual human activity profile is compared with the occupation human activity bank and the computer emits another new set of occupations. The computer may not allow occupations that repeat to run through the process twice as they could distort or slant the profile. Programmer's however may find value and allow repeats.

12. The new occupations are also reduced to human activities, that are viewed and the like, preferred or qualified human activities that survive are merged with the human activity profile list. Again those most often appearing at the top and on down. (This process we will refer to as winnowing; the ancient method of tossing grain chaff into the air and allowing the wind to blow away the undesirable chaff.) In this instance we will keep the desirable human activities and eliminate the undesirable activities.

13. The winnowing process continues until the individual profile stabilizes or there are no more significant changes in the occupations emitted by the computer.

14. The individual is now much more knowledgeable about their human activities and occupations and can scroll through the human activity library and select additional occupations

and reduce them to human activities to add to the list. This list change results in a new individual profile and when winnowed the computer emits new occupations.

15. The winnowing process again continues until there are no more significant changes in the occupations emitted by the computer. The surviving occupations we refer to as preliminary maxtalabilities.

16. The individual must now learn about, become involved with and be submitted to whatever exposure is available to the activities in the preliminary maxtalability occupations.

17. The talent discovery process is mostly positive, allowing occupations to winnow to the surface; but, final exposure to an occupation may be one of negative elimination. The elimination may be prevented if the offending people, places or things of an occupation can be altered to remove or neutralize the problem. Perhaps the computer programmers can set up the winnowing software to sub-divide all occupations to allow for alternate or sub-occupations and thus eliminate the need for exposure to any negative occupations. This may substantially increase the number of occupations in the profile.

18. This hands-on experience may eliminate some occupations, (preliminary maxtalabilities) because certain human activities involved in those occupations are no longer liked. Occupational exposure to activities will influence the individual so the individual can review the human activity list again to confirm, deny or otherwise adjust the position on the list of

certain activities. This would change the individual profile again. The individual can manually adjust up or down the activities on the human activity list. This will have the effect of again changing the profile.

19.   Each time the human activity profile list changes it will result in a new human activity profile. The winnowing continues until it stabilizes again and there are no more significant changes. The individual should now have identified a valuable group of maximum talent capabilities that can be used in work, hobby or recreation. Human activities not desirable in work may be acceptable or even desirable in a hobby or recreation.

Assuming there are an estimated 40,000 or more occupations, just one-tenth of a percent of an individual's top maxtalabilities amounts to 40 occupations to explore and choose from.

This maxtalability identity provides no guarantee that an individual can immediately exercise a talent, it only shows the best and most efficient opportunity to learn, experience and ultimately exercise a natural talent to the maximum. The individual now has the best of all occupations to work with, so much more than they ever had before. The individual is no longer wandering in the dark . . . the rest is up to the individual.

The (Maxtalability) Winnowing Process
(Does not include possible use of job task profiles.)

ALL OCCUPATIONS ARE REDUCED TO JOB TASKS
I
ALL JOB TASKS ARE REDUCED TO HUMAN ACTIVITIES
I
ALL HUMAN ACTIVITIES ARE VIEWED AND THE PREFERRED SELECTED
_____
I

A human activity list is created with the most often repeated on top
I
A human activity profile is created from this list
I   Occupation Human Activity
_____ Profile Bank of Occupations
                        I

           Human activity profile is run across the OHAPB
                       I
           Computer emits seven (arbitrary) occupations
                       I
              _____
              I

       New occupations are reduced to job tasks
               I
       New job tasks are reduced to human activities
               I
       New human activities are viewed and the preferred selected
           _____
       I

New preferred human activities merged into the human activity list
I
A human activity profile is created from the merged list
I   Occupation Human Activity
_____ Profile Bank of Occupations
                    I

           Human activity profile is run across the OHAPB
                       I
           Computer emits seven (arbitrary) occupations
                       I
              _____
              I

       New occupations are reduced to job tasks
               I
       New job tasks are reduced to human activities
               I
       New human activities are viewed and the preferred selected
           _____
       I

New preferred human activities merged into the human activity list = new profile...et.

The human activity winnowing process is repeated until the OHAPB bank no longer emits new occupations. We then have a preliminary occupation list to be experienced. When the preliminary occupations are experienced this will initially eliminate some occupations, this forces re-evaluation of the effected human activities that change the human activity list. The winnowing process is then re-run.

PART III

✦ ✦ ✦

IN SUPPORT OF
TALENT DISCOVERY

All people could achieve eminence in something
if only they knew what they excelled at.
BALTASAR GRACIAN,
TRANSLATED BY CHRISTOPHER MAUER

21

The Talent Discovery Booth & Virtual Reality

To discover talent we must initiate bold new methods, based on sound theory and applied with imagination and practical ingenuity.
JOHN M. STALNAKER, THE DISCOVERY OF TALENT

The following is a way, but not necessarily the only way, to search for the talent of an individual. Now that we have gone through the concept, lets enter a sample booth so that we can get a feel for a hands on experience.

Occupational Questionnaire

In preparation for using the talent discovery booth, the individual will complete a questionnaire designed to determine their likes, dislikes and indifference to specific occupations and activities. As an example, questions would be asked about prior work experiences, education background, recreational activities, and dreams. Additional occupations can be uncovered by the individual scrolling through a list of occupations he/she may have had some knowledge of in the past.

The Talent Discovery Booth (an example)

The individual will sit in front of a computer with either four monitors or one large monitor divided into four picture frames. This
user-friendly computer should be designed so the subject cannot
err. All instructions are in order of use with the next instruction
highlighted on the monitor. Keys to be used will light-up in proper
order, thereby acting as "flags" for the user.

I am more familiar with Apple Macintosh using Microsoft Word
and an arrow curser instead of depending on the keyboard. IBM
has made greater use of the key board. For the sake of those who are
not computer literate, we will refer to the key board keys.

In the beginning, it would be helpful to attend a introductory
class, have a counselor available to assist the person in the booth, or
at least to have assistance available via a telephone connection inside the booth.

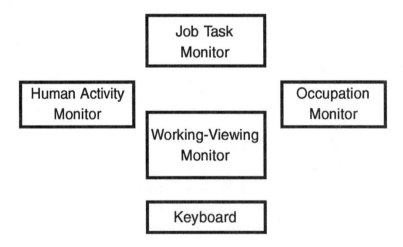

Occupations from the Questionnaire and tests.

The booth's power is turned on. The viewing or lower center screen
instructs the individual which keys or buttons need to be pushed to
indicate his/her answers to the questionnaire and tests, or instead of

buttons using a courser arrow as Apple Computer uses. The questionnaire and test questions could be both multiple choice and preference, are answered by pushing the appropriate buttons. (Many existing interest and career tests are already on computer.)

Once the questionnaire and test is completed the list of best occupations (let's say an arbitrary seven of each) appears on the right-side of the screen. These fourteen occupations will appear on the right monitor and automatically converted to job tasks that will appear on the center overhead monitor with the job tasks appearing most often positioned at the top of the list. In some occupations the job tasks might need to be broken down into sub-job tasks.

(There may be value for the individual to also see audio visuals of the job tasks. The computer programmers who develop the talent discovery program can decide if job tasks should play a more important role in talent discovery.)

The job tasks are automatically converted to human activities which will appear on the right-side of the left monitor waiting to be viewed.

The bottom center monitor is the working and viewing screen. The viewing screen would have the usual start, restart or frame stop controls to allow the viewer maximum versatility in visual reviewing a human activity. (This screen can also be used to view an occupation, or job task).

With a push of a lighted key, the first human activity on the human activity waiting list will appear on the monitor. The person will experience an audio visual of the activity. There could be four buttons labeled like, indifferent, dislike and mistake. Upon viewing the visual of each human activity the computer will prompt the individual for a response: either like, indifferent or dislike. If the like button is pushed the activity will be added to the human activity list on the left side of the human activity monitor. If the individual pushes the wrong button by mistake they can push the mistake button and then push the proper button.

As the human activities from the human activities waiting list are viewed the likes appear on a list on the left side of the left monitor with those most often repeated positioned at the top of the list.

The indifferent and dislike human activities will drop-off the human activity list (although computer programmers may find dislikes to be of value in comparison of individual profiles to occupational profiles.)

When all the human activities on the waiting list have all been viewed and is vacant, the computer automatically creates a profile from the human activity profile list and runs the profile across the occupation human activity profile bank. The computer processes the information, and the new occupations that best match the first stage individual profile appear on the right side of the screen of the right screen.

The computer program can be designed to highlight only the profiles that match up to 70%, 80% or higher; or to highlight a minimum number of occupations (let's say seven). The seven new occupations will go through the same process: changing each occupation to job tasks that join the job task list, and then reducing the job tasks to human activities that will go onto the human activity waiting list. These new activities will be viewed and the like human activities will be merged with the human activity profile list, with the most often repeated activities positioned at the top of the list; and a new profile will be created.

This will be done again and again until the computer can make no further significant changes and we have a list of preferred occupations or maxtalabilities in order of percentage of match to the individual. These maxtalabilities will appear on the monitor and the booth emits a print out of them, including in-depth information as to how and where to get information and help to experience the maxtalabilities.

New occupations will be added to the human activity viewing bank as necessary; the viewing bank will probably go through many stages of refinement to provide more depth and efficiency of talent discovery. Each addition, change or refinement may result in a beneficial change in individual profiles.

After participating in Talent Discovery the individual should consider the highest matched maxtalability occupations. If the individual needs help, a counselor could be consulted. (Talent Discovery counseling could become a new profession!)

Talent Discovery will uncover computer programmers and those persons who are talented in profile development, who in turn will help develop methods to further simplify and improve the discovery process. At this stage we should be in the maxtalability ball park where investigative study, experience, exposure and participation will continue to refine an individual's understanding of his/her capabilities.

As the individual watches the progression on the computer, he/she will discover things about him/herself they never knew before. They will see their strengths and weaknesses and where their talents best fit in the many occupations. Now they can focus on pursuing their maxtalabilities from a position of knowledge and strength.

Ordinary people will find an easy affinity with the human activity concept, for it has always been a part of our daily activity. Although the Talent Discovery process is new, most human activities are quite old and natural to all humans.

People Change

As previously stated, when subjecting their maxtalabilities to study, observation and actual experience people will have to leave the computer. At the end of the initial (and all future) booth experiences the booth computer emits a print out and breakdown of the last human activity list, profile and maxtalabilities and an identification number is issued. With exposure people may change their mind about some of the human activities on their list and may decide to eliminate or give a higher priority to certain activities, resulting in a new profile and new maxtalabilities for them to experience. In order to re-enter the previous matching the individual will need access to their previous talent discovery booth experiences by the use of the identification number. (Or hand print?)

With this identification number individuals can get back into the computer to access their previous information and continue recreating their profile as they experience and learn. As years pass people mature and undergo genetic changes. This ongoing development results in a profile change, sometimes only slightly and other times drastically. Some people may alter or stay in one or more occupation all of their lives, others may change occupations several times.

Many middle-aged people suddenly find the career they loved and found challenging is no longer satisfying or fulfilling; they don't know why or what to do about it. Continuing exposure to the computer will provide warning of change. It is best to be prepared to know this is happening and to know what to do about it. Finding a new maxtalability may be more interesting and challenging.

A person's thought patterns, physical capabilities and senses are key factors in the winnowing process. Time and experience will change these and most likely alter their profile.

As people become used to their profiles they will grow with them, know when something might affect or change it, and run a new profile. A new genetic phase may tell the individual that an occupational change is necessary to preserve their vitality, health, and longevity. Circumstances may dictate that a profile be done annually (or more frequently), especially for maturing and developing students.

Other Profiles

Through Talent Discovery leisure time interests may be discovered;

interests that better fit an individual's lifestyle, emotions and health, resulting in maximum enjoyment. One day a program may be designed to find additional profiles, such as personal fulfillment, life purpose, contribution to humanity or other objectives. Different profiles can be developed to span every area of an individual's life including where an individual should live and compatible mate selection.

The Mind - To Know Itself

Through the booth exercise, individuals will continue to learn more about themselves. The objective is to find the best environment to go along with the best occupation.

Gordon Taylor in his book, *The Natural History of the Mind*, describes how the mind participates: "The brain seems to be constantly checking what it sees against what it has on record, to see if a match can be made."

The individual's mind can help in the winnowing process as it observes what is happening. For the first time the mind will be free to roam in a familiar landscape of its own genetic capabilities where it can learn, try, experience and create in its own way and time. It is possible efficient talent genes, once awakened, will further enrich maxtalabilities.

Virtual Reality

Virtual reality programs can be developed to simulate actual experiences in all activities, especially sensitive occupations, such as surgery, diamond cutting or high diving.

In Michael Heim's book, *The Metaphysics of Virtual Reality*, he says in his foreword: "Virtual reality is the technology that can be applied to every human activity. It is the first intellectual technology that permits the active use of the body in the search for knowledge."

Virtual reality allows an individual to experience an activity a step removed from actual experience. An individual will be able to experience an activity from the inside and observe it from the outside, as the individual's senses come into vivid play. There has to be a greater value in using artificial experience, compared to visuals. There is no doubt that virtual reality is the ultimate in sensing.

Current virtual reality devices consisting of control gloves and head-mounted displays would add complication and cost to the Talent Discovery booth, but they would also be worth it. Using a full-room tele-presence, instead of gloves and head-mounted displays, would change the structure of the talent booth even more. In the United States, Japan and Europe commitments are already underway to make virtual reality more effective and less complicated.

There is no doubt that virtual reality can enrich perception, giving the individual a stronger feel than visuals. Virtual reality technology could be a present or a future advance in Talent Discovery. Three dimensional visuals may be another step closer to actual experience. Perhaps each one may be efficient for certain classes of activities. Time, cost and availability will indicate their use.

Virtual reality cannot only simulate human activities and actions but it could speed up the process of talent discovery. One day virtual reality may also speed up activity exposure time.

Talent Discovery development may have to go through two steps: the first using audio visuals and the second using virtual reality, when a virtual reality activity library is complete and available for all human activities. Talent Discovery would be substantially enriched and more efficient if the virtual reality human activity library was ready when the first booth was opened; though I do not know if such a library is practical or within our grasp at this time.

Virtual reality is here and belongs in the education system. It will become a future tool of teaching and learning to select not only maxtalabilities but to improve the quality of education.

Learning Sources and Marketing Your Talent

We don't need to worry about having enough sources for researching our maxtalabilities. There will be many companies competing to provide software for the booth that will provide in-depth sources and learning information, as computer networking already accomplishes. Individuals will have a variety of occupational possibilities available to them. As an example:

1. They may be able to select the time, place, and environment in which to learn more about maxtalability talents. Such as:
   A. What responsibility to accept
   B. What people if any to work with
   C. Where you want to work
   D. When you want to work
   E. How you want to work (full or part-time)an ideal working environment can enhance talent creativity and problem solving ability.

2. Locate companies you may want to work for from a master occupational list on the computer. (Call them and ask for an interview). You can also register your talent and they will call you or a talent group may want you to join them.

3. Through a computer network, contact others with similar talents and create learning groups.
   A. Work individually or with a partner
   B. Create problem-solving think tanks
   C. Create service companies
   D. Create consulting companies

   Individuals with undeveloped or newly-discovered talents who desire to serve as a think tank member would probably be in demand to solve company problems all over the country in their maxtalability field. Without prior knowledge or experience these talents could provide a fresh approach that would enhance old products or create new products, markets or services, at the same time individuals or groups are learning studying or training their one or more chosen maxtalabilities.

4. There may be talents to utilize in hobbies, sports and entertainment, both as a participant and as an observer. Such groups can also be formed.

5. Educational institutions will offer instruction on specific talents. A list of institutions will no doubt be on the computer. I can visualize the future when schools will have activity labs for every occupation to support their curriculum subjects, where students can experience hands-on activities over and over again exposing them to maximum sensibility, thereby forcing boredom or challenge.

6. Existing professional organizations will subdivide, according to specific talents and become more influential in our society. Until now professional associations existed mostly to service those in the profession. After talent discovery, these same associations could have a stronger influence in the education of their future professionals and become a better support profession for it.

They will become available across the country to provide help, guidance, education and work connections for people with newly-discovered talents who are in need of their services. Talent groups will work together to find ways to educate, develop and market their talents. Thousands of new, professional organizations will spring up and new businesses will be started to service these organizations.

Creating the Perfect Job and Selling it to Companies

Instead of only finding the best job that fits, the computer can create the perfect job or occupation from an individual's profile of preferred activities. This process could include the creation of new occupations by combining preferred activities into a new occupation that would have an economic value in the marketplace.

There is no doubt Talent Discovery will change the makeup of occupations and professions to fit the talent activities of people.

Business Will Change

Business is changing. Huge corporations will no longer use large buildings and maintain extensive in-house staffs, rather they will subcontract jobs out to talent groups. Let me cite an example: a company needs to solve a problem, improve a product or develop a new product. They place a price of $500,000 on the project and present their needs to an appropriate talent guild. The guild places it on their bulletin board. Individuals or complete think tanks will decide to try and solve the company's needs.

You and the other members of your think tank meet and come up with a solution. Your think tank submits the idea to the talent guild. If your idea is accepted by the company your think tank receives $475,000 divided between each think tank member) and the talent guild receives $25,000 (or 5%) for its services. Or perhaps only a part of your idea is used. Then your think tank receives only $100,000 (less 5% to the guild). If you feel a solution is worth more than $500,000 you patent royalties for seventeen years. This could help level out all incomes.

If your think tank's idea is not used, the idea could go into the talent guild's bank of ideas for another company to use in the future; though it is still the property of your think tank. The guild might also employ salesman who market the guild's products to companies, some of the products belonging to your talent think tank.

It would be a simple task to set up a think tank of fresh talent, even for the smallest company in every industry. Once unleashed, nothing would be able to compete with the synergistic power of a think tank of highly talented, industry-targeted people. That is the power of talent genetics. "Out of the mouth of babes?" Woe to those companies who do not believe.

Qualifying Entrepreneurs

The computer can also help discover if a person should be in business for him/herself, work alone or work with or for others. People who desire their own business will know if they are capable and if they have the talent and temperament to do so.

Rather than selecting and starting a business with no known factors, they now can do so with strong support information, allowing them the maximum potential for success, rather than facing the 10% survival rate of new businesses today.

Patents

People will love and enjoy their maxtal jobs and be more creative. A whole world of uncovered talents could open the door to a multitude of new inventions. There is no doubt the patent offices will be inundated with a flood of new inventions emerging from this treasury of newly-discovered maximum talent capabilities.

Inventions for new products and improvements to existing products could open up new markets, making products and services less expensive for consumers. A country that had a six-month lead into the realm of new inventions could have an economic head start that would make it a world leader for generations.

22

Tools for Talent Discovery

If a man has talent and cannot use it, he has failed.
If a man has talent and uses only half of it, he has
partly failed. If a man has talent and somehow
learns to use the whole of it, he has gloriously
succeeded, and won the satisfaction and a triumph
few men ever know.
THOMAS CLAYTON WOLFE, THE WEB AND THE ROCK

The Talent Discovery method can be compared to an automobile engine: all of the parts must fit in close tolerance to each other to start the engine and for it to work efficiently. As with an automobile's engine the efficiency level of Talent Discovery will depend upon the development and efficiency of the parts and tools used to make it work.

With the use of computer technology we will be able to develop a method of talent discovery. Computer programmers are the professionals who will ultimately tell us what tools and what steps will be required to develop the most efficient Talent Discovery process.

At this early stage of development, the following tools appear to be what are needed. The following is a method (but not necessarily the only method) of talent discovery:

Talent Discovery Tools

1.   Expand, code and number the present Department of Labor Dictionary of Occupations to cover all distinct occupations; and then transfer this revised information onto computer software. The most recent edition of the Department of Labor Dictionary of Occupational Titles (DOT), published in 1977, took years to develop. Although the DOT lists over 20,000 occupations, substantial revision, updating and expansion will be necessary to produce the distinct list of occupations necessary for Talent Discovery to determine maxtalabilities.

   For instance: DOT (code number) 041-101 lists Musician-Instrumental as one occupation. There are over one hundred different musical instruments, each one involving a different set of activities. Playing a violin and beating a drum are entirely different activities. In reality, the only common activity of musicians is reading music; and even that may not be required in all music performances. If there is only one musician occupation, what do we call a violinist? sub-musician occupation or a vocation? The same is true of lawyers and physicians and geologists as we previously examined. It is obvious there are decisions to be made and new categories need to be established.

   In other parts of the world there are occupations particular to a certain country; these should be reduced and included in the human activity library bank.

   It is not my intention to criticize the DOT listing of occupations. The DOT has been a great help to me in developing the 'Getting to Know You' exercise and the development of the Talent Discovery concept. The objective of the DOT system was to clarify and simplify occupations, which it has succeeded in doing. Because this search is for an individual's maximum talent capability through human activities a more definitive and in-depth breakdown of occupations is needed.

2. Catalogue, code and number all of the job tasks that exist in the estimated 40,000 plus occupations. Job tasks in many occupations may have to be broken down further into sub-job tasks. This information would then have to be transferred onto computer software, creating a job task library bank. It is necessary to develop a job task bank because job tasks need to be broken down to create the human activity bank.

3. Interpret each and all job tasks in terms of the human activities involved. The computer could do this break down automatically but there may be value in the individual seeing it happen and be able to witness job task visuals.

4. Catalogue, code and number all of the human activities involved in all of the job tasks of all the occupations; and then transfer the human activity catalogue onto computer software.

5. Create a human activity computer profile grid or bar code that will represent all occupations; each occupation profile created according to the human activity numbers and or codes used in that occupation. A human activity profile of all occupations would then be input onto a computer, becoming the human activity profile bank of occupations.

6. All human activities are placed on audio visuals that are also stored in the computer vi..eo library.

7. Create a common or standard human activity profile that will represent any individual, and will be compatible with the occupational human activity profile. Each individual profile is created according to the human activity numbers or bar codes found in an individual's maxtalabilities.

8. A computer is designed and developed to store and process the necessary programs needed for the Talent Discovery booth with the necessary monitors and equipment to accommodate the previous mentioned items. (If the computer capacity requirement is inconvenient or too large it may have to be linked to a central computer.) The computer contains the human activity video banks from which an individual can compare or run his/her profile across the occupation library so that the computer can select suitable occupations. The Talent Discovery booth, software and necessary networking should be available at as many locations as possible, so that it is available to everyone.

   The word booth indicates privacy. The process could be done with a group of individual's guided by a counselor but requires an individual's full and uninterrupted attention. However, the time to complete will vary for each individual.

9. If possible, adapt the Talent Discovery booth to utilize virtual reality systems. Creating and developing virtual reality for all occupations, job tasks and human activities would prove valuable; however it would be a massive undertaking and may delay the booth development.

10. Computer programs will have to be written to support and

run the Talent Discovery process and a network developed to integrate all the necessary software. When all the necessary tools are developed, Talent Discovery can proceed and the talent discovery booth can be made available.

Other Research and Actions to be Considered

If not a part of the original concept, research should start on related areas such as: environmental conditions an individual is exposed to and how these relate to human activities and thought patterns. Each human activity is responsive to people, places and things that reflect on the environmental personality of a human activity. We do not want to eliminate a talent where the human activity environment can be accommodated to suit an individual.

If we can develop and integrate these areas they may become additional factors in the qualification of talent identification and profile sharpness.

Can talent discovery research be done in some way other than an interrogation or elimination-response method? Only future research will provide the answer. Maybe submitting a person to certain drugs or measuring their brain waves or using a lie detector device will be used in the future.

If the substantial cost to build and make talent discovery a reality is beyond the capability of private enterprise, it may be necessary for the project to, at least originally, be sponsored by the government but not controlled, as is the Genome project. In time, taxes from profits created, income taxes from new talents, and savings in government dependency programs should more than pay for the Talent Discovery program. It would be better for private enterprise to float a bond issue and carry the talent discovery program to fruition.

There are many affluent business leaders who could merge their talents and pursue the completion of the Talent Discovery process.

I'm convinced they would find the results rewarding and very profitable. People like Lee Iacocca, Donald Trump, Bill Gates and Steven Jobs; along with financiers like Kirk Kerkorian and Warren Buffett could form a committee to get the job done and at the same time make a significant contribution to the people who helped them make their fortunes. A magnificent accomplishment, such as finding the key to discovering human talent, might be the true purpose of their talents and wealth, for which history would best remember them.

We spend billions of dollars on health care, welfare and unemployment benefits for vocational misfits; and almost nothing researching the cause and prevention of these problems. Now, with the use of Talent Discovery we can do something about it.

23

In Support of Every Individual Having Talent

Man must be educated to realize his greatness and
to become worthy of the powers that are his.
MARIA MONTESSORI

Talent is not a special attribute or trait that only certain people are born with, talent is a mental reaction to a specific interest, activity or series of activities that all of us possess. It is a condition that occasionally surfaces when an individual comes close to or is exposed to efficient capabilities they were born with.

A genius in one specific vocation, such as a violinist, cannot apply that same genius efficiency to a different vocation, such as genetics, and achieve equal results. If talent was a special gift only certain people were born with those people would be able to apply their genius to any or all areas of endeavor . . . and there is no evidence of such a person having ever lived or living now. Not being an exclusive trait, talent opens the possibility that any individual exposed to a specific activity or vocation may have talent ability that will surface. Therefore it is safe to assume that every individual is born with talent capability in some unknown area. If we can find talent in each individual, it would be the great leveler needed to support self esteem in all people.

Ability-A Human Trait

The makeup of humankind suggests that we are all born with equal body parts and abilities, but the characteristics of those assets are unique to each individual; as is each leaf or snowflake. In all of our other faculties we seem to have been given equal capabilities, different but equal. No one has been born with the advantage of an eye in the back of their head or three arms. Therefore, why would one person have talent capability and others not? The fact that we do not know an individual's talent is not proof that talent is nonexistent.

Those who disagree would have difficulty proving all humans do not have equal maximum talent capability. The fact that every individual has a high level of ability in some area appears to be a natural trait of all humans.

Talent Survival

The Talent Discovery concept suggests there is evidence that every normal individual was born with or possesses some high level of talent capability. Many species of animals have become extinct in the last few hundred years, mostly for environmental reasons, although a dominant or superior species usually survives. Evolutionists may tell us that sub-intelligence humans would not have survived. Equal abilities may be necessary to prevent the splitting of the human race into a super and a sub-culture. A high level of talent ability (even talent that is not exposed) and its use may be a necessary trait for survival of humanity.

If only a select class of people had talent capabilities an elite structure would arise, and those persons not so endowed would be reduced to permanent servitude; this has not happened.

At one time it was assumed that certain races and women were not capable of equal ability or intelligence as others. We now know that this is not true. The same misinterpretation could be true of talent capability.

Heredity can play a role; however a high level of talent can be born from seemingly untalented parents, and talented parents can produce untalented children. The obvious conclusion is that talent can pop up in the most unlikely places, at any time. This being the case, talent may be there in all of us, just waiting for the right environment to grow and bloom.

This is not proof, but it does indicate that talent is not predictable; it is random and appears to be everywhere, only waiting for an opportunity in which to come forth.

Success

I have watched people gain success, people who should not have become successful. They had nothing going for them, not family, education or money. I saw them go from nothingness to towers of confidence and strength, perhaps initiated by a strong ambition exposed to opportunity. They may not have been in their most efficient talent area but the motivation was strong enough for them to succeed in an area in which they could excel. The ability to succeed was there, waiting for an opportunity. Imagine what they might have done if that same motivation had been applied to their true talent capability. The result would be considered a maximum talent performance.

Although our maxtalability may not be known, the power of motivation to succeed is there, to support it when it is found. It is possible there lurks behind each of us the ability to come out of our shells and to attain top talent capability with built-in motivation to support a maximum talent capability if and when it is discovered.

Geniuses

Great inventors and scientists prove the existence of talent; though they are but simple men. Thomas Edison and Ben Franklin would be the first to agree. Edison said that genius is one percent inspiration and ninety-nine percent perspiration. Like Einstein, Ben Franklin failed in school and was expelled. He was totally self taught.

If Edison, Einstein and Franklin are simple people, like the rest of us, with little in their personal makeup to indicate a dominant potential, then talent may be a natural capability of all people. Scientists have examined Einstein's brain to see if it was different from other people's. The conclusion was Einstein's brain had an unusually bumpy surface (or more nodules) compared to other human brains. They may be right, but did the unusual nodules result in genius or did genius result in the nodules? In Einstein's teens he was told by his teacher that he should leave school because he would never be a good student nor amount to anything. Were the nodules present at that time?

Geniuses are not complimented when they are called genius; they consider "genius" an abnormality and they would rather not be so referred. For many geniuses it has been a burden too heavy to carry; often resulting in emotional trauma and even self destruction. Most geniuses are quite humble and thankful for their talent and many have said that other people too might be talented at something given the right opportunity.

Is there another Einstein living in the wilds of Africa, New Guinea or Mongolia who does not have the opportunity to learn how to read or write and thus will never discover if he/she is a genius?

Some people believe there are different degrees of intelligence among people. Is this belief brought on by society over-selling education and using education to set intelligence standards? I do not doubt formal education is a substantial asset but I believe education is a tool to use intelligence, not intelligence itself.

Talented people are simple but dedicated people who have had the good fortune to have their talents surface, perhaps by accident and in a convenient or fertile environment. All people are capable of high talent in some area that can surface when exposed to a compatible and fertile environment.

The Eyes

Can we penetrate the neuron structure to find out what an individual's talent is? Is it in a certain section of the brain or is it a combination of neuronic impulses connecting across many areas? We do not as yet know this. What we do know is that every person has interests that light-up their eyes. We can only draw the conclusion this reaction is the result of a person's imagination visualizing an interest, pleasurable action or thought. Can we go about lighting-up every one's eyes and finding their talent interests? Some of this light may be touching neurons that relate not only to desires but to natural talents or abilities. The "eyes light-up" interest indicates that every individual's brain or genetic structure has the ability to become excited and interested about something.

Work Stress

If you are highly successful by determination and ambition rather than through natural talent you may have activated certain self-destructive genes within your system. The proof is in the growing sales of antacids, pain relievers, etc. Your work can ruin your health. If we can retain only those activities that the individual enjoys doing and is capable at, then the destructive forces may not be active.

It is healthful, productive, profitable and fulfilling to work in areas you enjoy and are capable at. There is no doubt there are such activities for each of us; activities compatible with our individual well being.

Superior Genes

The difference in each of us is that our genes are dominant or superior in certain traits. The same principle may apply to our talent personality, which is also probably genetically engineered. Our personality influences how we look, act and think.

We can see how a person looks and acts, however we cannot see an individual's interests, thoughts or know what a person's abilities are. Talent personality is expressed in our interests and is subject to the level of comfort we feel toward areas that are of interest.

Superior genes in talent personality may be well hidden, which begs the question: will they find talent genes in the gene mapping program? If they can be found, will we be able to measure the efficiency of a particular gene, gene cluster or controller genes to identify them as highly efficient or superior? Talent appears to be a necessary building block of the DNA. Each have a complete genetic code with more efficient genes in some compatible sets of activities. All people have a talent capability.

The Source of Talent Genes

Ultimately they may find talent genes. Geneticists have discovered our gene bank consists mostly of junk genes; genes they bypass in the Genome mapping program. Junk genes may also be the source of talent genes that are inactive in most of us. Genes are evidently turned on and off, either by internal influence, external exposure or environment. Maybe this is why some people suddenly come to life when given opportunities that appeal to them.

Rather than individual talent genes, the source of talent may be efficient talent gene groupings working together synergistically. Understanding how genes work together may one day expose talent. Having a potential source of talent genes is further indication that talent genes in some way or combination may exist.

Why Talent is not Obvious

Outward appearances do not indicate talent. Talent is not a physical characteristic that can be seen. Other than body building (that may not be a true talent) there is no physical or mental difference shown by talented people when they are exercising their talent other than the talent itself. All the more reason to believe that each of us could be talented at something. Maximum talent capability may not be apparent in all of us because not all of us are privileged to be exposed to the necessary activity and fertile environment in which all four areas (interest, physical ability, sense, and mental acceptance) are compatible and needed for talent to function efficiently.

In most of us, talent is deeply buried because there is no way that each of us can be exposed to the 40,000 plus occupations, and their varied activities, to locate our best talent. When it does surface, talent is found in a wide variety of people; therefore there is no reason to believe that talent is limited to certain people or segments of society.

We Have Been Wrong Before

At one time people thought the earth was flat. Is it really so hard to believe each of us has a high talent trait? What is so special about the people who have realized their talents? They are just ordinary people. They don't have wings like angels and they go to the bathroom like we do. Were they just lucky to have been born in an environment that allowed their talent to come out and develop? They have no greater personal happiness than the rest of us.

I cannot prove that each of us has an equal set of talents in some area. It is as much of an assumption as: man being able to fly, the electric light bulb, mobile telephones or man walking on the moon; except this is much less of an assumption. We cannot afford to be stubborn about the fact that all individuals have a reservoir of untapped ability.

Individually my conclusions may not be adequate proof that all people have talent capability but together they are considerable evidence that should not be denied. Still I have questions.

Will it Work?

Now that the concept has been developed I am still cautious. At times it seems too unbelievable to be true. The concept has been developed but it has not been tested. Is it workable? What could go wrong? I feel reluctant to write a book about a new concept that has not been tested. Who can I turn to for help with this lack of confidence?

"How about me?"

"Henry? This is a confidence problem, not a concept problem."

"So. . . I'm a confidence man. That was a pun. Heh. . . heh. . . well? Sorry about that. I'm not limited to concept problems. What's your problem?" Henry inquires.

"Suddenly I question whether Talent Discovery will work." I admit.

"So you want me to play devil's advocate? Okay. Why do you have questions?"

"It's too fantastic to be true."

"So?"

"Well, there are so many things that have to be developed and come together just right."

"It doesn't have to come together just right. It will not be perfect in the beginning," Henry admits, "variable procedures using many different human procedures never are. We already agreed that it will work to some degree for any one individual. For example, maybe talent discovery will convince: an individual to quit drug trafficking to become a talented archeologist; a welfare mother to become a computer technician; a prison inmate to become a talented cancer researcher; an advertising executive who is six months away from a heart attack to switch to a job he enjoys and can live with; or a student to pursue a degree in which he can succeed at.

"How significant are these changes? You're only running an individual profile converted to code numbers across a bank of 40,000 human activity coded occupations. It's as simple as the old IBM card sort system. Except for the human activity viewing time spent, it's no more time consuming or complicated than a pin ball machine. It is far less complicated than running a fingerprint fragment across all the fingerprints on file; and that can be done in a few minutes. What Talent Discovery requires is basic computer programming."

"Yes, fingerprints would appear to be more complicated," I agreed. "But what if the person is not happy with any of the maxtalabilities he or she ends up with?"

"How can that be? Most everything they like and can do well is in their discovered maxtalabilities. Look, picture a long wall divided into one-inch squares, each square is labeled with one of 40,000 occupations. You, the worker are trying to find the right job or profession; or you, the student, are trying to decide on a course of study; you must put your finger on one of the labels to select the occupation that you can do best and is best for your health. How are you going to do it?"

"I might find one that I am interested in," I suggest.

"Interest is important in highlighting an occupation, but it is not qualified as healthful nor does it indicate capability that results in career or work success. How has interest reduced our drop out rate? Interest may not last and in time may turn to boredom or drudgery. How are individuals going to find an occupation through interest that will protect them from stress that effects physical, mental, emotional health, and longevity? How is a person going to find an occupation that generates life-long challenge, creativity and fulfillment? You might as well throw darts at the occupations on the wall, because that is what most people are now doing. How good is that process? I'll tell you . . . it stinks."

"Henry!"

"I'm sorry, but it's true. Through Talent Discovery an individual can come up with maxtalabilities and that is intelligent selection. Their chance of hitting a maxtalability with a dart is 40,000 to one. With Talent Discovery you don't have to throw darts, it takes the gamble out of choosing an occupation. An occupation selection not supported by qualified talent is placing the rest of your life and health in jeopardy and to make matters worse, in this age of restructuring there is less occupation security."

"Henry, did all that come out of you?"

"Sorry. I got carried away . . . a little."

"Will people want to go through the Talent Discovery process?" I ask.

"Would you want to take a chance of throwing darts at a wall when your healthy, qualified and potentially successful maxtalabilities can be found?"

"I guess not; but what if it doesn't work? Look at all the government programs that were supposed to work and don't."

"When private companies realize the profit potential of Talent Discovery it will work. They won't ask if it will work, they will find a way to make it work. That is their business. There may be a few bugs; but that won't stop them for long. There are no unknown factors, it is just deciding the best procedure to use. Look at how you overcame problems in your business. Did a few bugs ever stop you?" Henry challenged.

"I suppose you're right. You think someone can design a useful profile?"

"For computer programmers this is a simple bar or grid design; it is nothing compared to the fingerprint comparison and space probe programming. We are building a profile from an individual's positive activities. That has never been done before. This is a great move forward. How can we go wrong with it? Edison brought us light. Talent Discovery throws the light on talent to learn, work and live by."

"Henry. The light comparison is really good but I don't remember writing anything about that."

"Well, I just thought I'd throw that in."

"What if they can't develop a catalogue and therefore can't build an occupational converted to human activities bank?"

"The catalogue and coding has already been started by the Department of Labor in its Dictionary of 20,000 Occupations. It only needs to be expanded to your estimate of 40,000. And to some degree the department has already broken down occupations into job tasks. We are just going one step further, breaking down the job tasks into human activities. There is nothing to stop this from being done providing we find the people and obtain the finances to do it."

"What if an individual does not have enough positive human activities repeated often enough to create a meaningful profile?"

"People have been taking interest tests for fifty years," Henry replied. "We know by their answers that people have groups of preferences that repeat, no matter how many different ways a certain question is asked. Every human has an abhorrence/preference activity personality, no matter how many human activities there are the individual cannot deny preferred activities when they come up. The activities will come up because the individual is forcing activities to repeat in the winnowing process as the individual zeros in harder and stronger in the same activity areas. Winnowed often enough, activities have to repeat and profiles will emerge."

"What I hear you describe seems to come from a different point of view. Anyway, everything you say makes sense, but somehow I feel uneasy about releasing the information."

"My friend. It is not a question of 'will it work?' You have developed the framework so that it can be made to work. Intricate procedures are not perfect in the beginning; things change as they are assembled and improved upon as they are used. Compare the personal computers of today with the initial monsters of twenty years ago.

"No one can deny that your work has awakened the world to possibilities and methods that can improve the lives of everyone. You are a perfectionist and expect this complicated and involved procedure to work perfectly the first time. Be content with the principles you have established, sit back, and enjoy watching it evolve, develop and mature.

"What is your real problem? Are you afraid to release this information because you know it will disturb your quiet, retired existence? Is that it? You can't do this anonymously you know. You hatched this egg; now you're going to have to nurture it into existence. Your knowledge will be needed. No one apparently has the research background you have experienced or knows what you and your mind knows about Talent Discovery." Blip.

He answered my questions. So here it is. Now the responsibility to see Talent Discovery come into fruition is in your many hands and voices. The powers that be will have to listen to you, if you care enough.

24

The Benefits

*Finding the talented, encouraging their
advancement, making known their potentials,
serves two purposes: individuals are helped to
fulfill their promise, and society is enriched.*
DAEL WOLFE, THE DISCOVERY OF TALENT

The benefits of Talent Discovery, from a different perspective, are:

✦ to improve the health, happiness, purpose and well-being of all people, including: those who are educable, those who are not educable, employed and unemployed workers, retirees, and people who are dependent or disabled.

✦ to provide government, business and industry with highly talented and creative individuals who can discover ways to solve and prevent personal and sociological problems.

✦ to give all people the opportunity to find their maximum talent capability in occupations, hobbies and recreation; allowing for the best quality of life.

No one can guarantee that everyone will be an overnight success; but, if government leaders, businessmen and educators collaborate to make Talent Discovery work, everyone will find a valuable benefit.

How can Talent Discovery not benefit all people when:

- ✦ Millions of new talents will be discovered.

- ✦ People will go off welfare and begin to pay taxes rather than being on the dole.

- ✦ Some criminals may find other talents and valuable occupations; thereby decreasing crime and its negative affects on society.

- ✦ Refocused middle-aged workers will be able to resurrect their careers with new talents.

- ✦ New discoveries and inventions will come forth, resulting in new industries and jobs.

- ✦ People will lead less stressful lives and relieve health care costs.

- ✦ Students will find successful career directions.

Parents and Children

Much is written about the deterioration of personal and family values in our society. Discovered talent can open up a positive flow of communication between parents and their children. Parents can provide informed guidance and look for ways to enhance their children's natural talents rather than blindly focusing their children towards incompatible occupations. Parents can ask questions, suggest subjects, and be on the lookout for references to the child's interests such as gifts that support talent.

Is there another way to help all people? Everyone who goes through the Talent Discovery program will learn valuable information about themselves; more than they could ever know otherwise.

The New Frontier

It was the immigrants' desire for land and opportunity that overcame the dangers of America's west. Many inventions and some of the largest companies in America were built by immigrants.

During recent government debates, many of our elected officials favored immigration. Immigrants are imaginative, hard working and bring renewed vitality to our country; while many of our natural born citizens are self-satisfied. In our free environment, immigrants seem to strive on challenge.

Can we open up a new frontier that will challenge all of our citizens and give them something new to strive for, something each individual can get excited about, a positive life-long challenge?

There are numerous books written on self-esteem, self worth and personal identity. These attributes, however, are difficult to attain and maintain without a foundation of capability in some area. Talent is the one capability that each individual may possess that can create self-esteem and personal value and identity.

Discovering new talents is the only frontier most individuals have left. How can we deny them this? Will people care about discovering their hidden talents? How can you help but believe it? Look around you. When people care about something that is of interest, is satisfying or a challenge, they will want it with a vengeance. Look how they fight, argue and spend endless time and money on frivolous things that are fleeting and unimportant, imagine how they would fight, argue and spend endless time pursuing something as valuable as their own talent.

Talent Discovery will expose millions of the most highly-talented people in pin-pointed subjects the world has never known. This has never happened before. How can we begin to imagine the effect this will have?

I imagine you are thinking: "So what, we have many talented people in those areas." This is my point: we don't and have never had the vast power of multitudes of synergistically talented groups of people. The evidence is obvious. Our problems started, grew, and are now out of control. The purpose of Talent Discovery is to find highly-talented people in each problem field who are now working at jobs completely unrelated to their hidden maximum talent to solve those problems.

Talent is Ageless

The world of work has changed dramatically in just the last generation. Occupations split and split again. They grow more technical, specialized and demanding. Job security has fallen victim to restructuring and downsizing. A person's abilities must be continually updated to keep up with the fast pace of technology.

As we grow older the pace becomes more grinding. In past generations older workers had the needed knowledge and experience and were considered to be valuable employees. Today their knowledge and experience depreciate quickly and young recruits get their jobs. The older worker's self esteem and personal value has taken a terrible beating by demeaning and low paying jobs or the unemployment line.

Fortunately changes over the last few generations have expanded the number of ccupations to over 40,000; allowing for much greater latitude for more definitive talent use and application.

The Younger Generation

I was dismayed to find how many college students (often just before graduation) realized they were in the wrong major. I saw girls in tears, guys pacing back and forth and shaking their heads in disbelief, fully committed to student loans with no more time or money to re-focus their education. How could they possibly tell their parents about their realization? How would they sleep that night, after graduation and hearing all of the congratulations? What would they see in the mirror in the morning?

I often wonder how many college students have similar experiences. The student suicide rate is cause for alarm.

We owe more to these young people than we are now giving. Louis Perelman in his book Schools Out says that education has not invested in research to advance education.

Education needs to develop new ideas and innovations for people to learn in this highly technical age.

The Generation in Between

Having interviewed thousands of people for specific jobs, both those out of work and those seeking a change, there is no doubt in my mind that we have lost generations of people who cannot find a suitable career. Restructuring has created chaos in the lives of all classes of people. Their only option is to find some specific talent in their makeup, something salable.

Every new factory replaces workers with automation and robotics; and in business, entire departments are often replaced by outside service providers.

There are armies of disillusioned people who need to develop new talents. We have nothing to offer them. We are entering an age of specialization in which only individual maximum talent capability will provide security.

The Older Generation-Summer 1991

At my high school's fiftieth anniversary, each person was asked to stand-up and say a few words. One classmate (who I did not recognize) stood up, identified himself, and said: "My wife and I have two married children and four grandchildren. I am retired. We took a trip out west last year; and other than that I'm just sitting around waiting to die."

I felt so sorry for him. People have told me how fortunate I am to be excited and interested in something I really care about at my age. Medical research tells us that people who have an important purpose in life live longer and healthier lives. More and more people are taking early retirement and drift aimlessly. Talent Discovery could help retirees find a new purpose and help them feel of value. People with talent would become productive and continue to be instead of a cost to society.

We are doing something very wrong by letting our senior citizens expire without utilizing their wisdom and experience. Newly-discovered talents in retirement planning could add meaningful value to health, happiness and fulfillment.

All Generations

A few generations ago people did not know and were in awe of the talented, as though they had special gifts from God. The media has now brought "the stars" into our homes and lives; they are more common and familiar to us. People are starting to suspect that talent is more common.

For lack of a recognizable talent people may resort to less desirable means of identity. Our identity is our self esteem and self respect. If people have low self esteem it is easier for them to put on a false front, they may resort to crime or hide behind drug abuse. These are not good choices.

Talent Discovery can bring initiative and vitality to every person's life. People won't have to try to appear special, because with talent they are special. Talent discovery opens up a world of opportunities for honest identity. Talent is a positive internal value that creates value and pride. It is difficult to be dishonest with talent, because negative influence restricts the performance of talent.

The value in talent is in the performance of doing something the best we can. People who value themselves are more likely to be honest, ethical and decent. Discovered individual talent provides a positive way to live, the reward is self esteem and self respect.

The Talent Discovery concept bears a substantial responsibility. When one thinks about it carefully, this principle is far reaching and potentially could change the lives of everyone and everything in our world.

25

Questions and Answers

The hardest part is asking the right questions.
Why should the universe exist at all? The
explanation must be so simple and so beautiful
that when we see it we will all say 'how could it
have been otherwise?'
JOHN A. WHEELER, PHYSICIST, *READER'S DIGEST*

Question: Where will I find a Talent Discovery booth?

Answer: I presume talent discovery booths will be located in high schools, libraries, city halls, manufacturing plants, shopping centers, etc. Once government, education and business realize how profitable talent discovery can be, the booths will become even more accessible. In time the concept may become so simple that the software could be accessed at home on a personal computer.

Question: What will it cost?

Answer: If government decides talent eliminates or drastically reduces expensive government programs and results in a substantial increase in tax revenues, the use of the talent discovery booth may be free. If not there may be a charge that will be a pittance compared to the value received.

Question: What if I use the booth once a year and I find my maxtalabilities have changed. Will I have to change my work?

Answer: It is your choice. It is possible to reduce one talent to a hobby status or you might develop a talent that compliments a number of occupations which you may have to investigate. You may have only one fixed talent or you may be a multi-talented person. This is what Talent Discovery is all about: finding out what talents you want to use at every stage of life. You may be a person that needs or prefers diversification or change.

Question: Won't change hurt me financially?

Answer: You are in control now. You know what your talents are, what you want to do and when you want to do it. You now have known, salable talents to exercise as you desire or need.

Question: What if I have three top talents and I like them all?

Answer: Find a way to use them through professional organizations, or start your own company providing services to three different professions, or work with different talent groups.

Question: Where will I learn about my talent?

Answer: Through formal instruction at school or on closed circuit or educational TV channels. Providing resources for specific talents will become big business. When you register your talent, professional organizations will actively solicit you and help you locate education and employment sources. When the computer gives you your maxtalabilities it will provide you with this information.

Question: Will schools change the way they teach?

Answer: It is much easier to wrap the three R's around an individual's talent than it is to do what John W. Gardner referred to as "stuffing the three R's into students like sausages." Educators should welcome a natural learning direction to improve teaching and learning. Wouldn't talented instructors teaching talented and interested students be a change for the better?

Question: Will the government want to make educational changes?

Answer: I don't see why not. Discovered talent has a triple value: It provides new talent to solve government problems, it reduces government expense, and produces more tax revenues.

Question: What kind of people and organizations should have the job of developing Talent Discovery?

Answer: Educators, government leaders (Departments of Labor, Education, Health and Welfare), career consultants, cognitive engineers, businessmen, geneticists, robotics specialists, computer programmers (soft and hardware), and virtual reality specialists to name a few.

Question: Won't this booth process be long, drawn out and boring?

Answer: No way will it be boring. How can watching your talents emerge and finding out about yourself be dull? Can finding talents you will enjoy all of your life and be respected for be boring? How can discovering talents, occupations and hobbies that will allow you to lead a satisfying life not be of interest? For the first time individuals will have the opportunity to discover things about themselves they have never known before. In the future, finding talents may be the most important consideration of every person's life. It could be the meaning and expression of life.

Question: Won't Talent Discovery be a time-consuming process?

Answer: The computer does it faster than you might think, and engineers and programmers will improve upon its speed. How much time do you spend at school and at work, frustrated, dreaming, worrying, and doing tasks you were not designed to do? How much of your life do you spend on the wrong activities for naught? Any improvement is a substantial improvement.

Question: Will everyone have to go through it?

Answer: No. Only if you choose to. For those introduced to Talent Discovery it will be fun and full of surprises. It will be like opening a fortune cookie or finding the greatest treasure of all. Future generations will grow with talent discovery. It will be used throughout school . . . throughout life as it continues to unfold slowly, with new interests and challenges.

Question: Will I be a better person for finding my talent?

Answer: I would think you would be. If you understand that true talent is a responsibility; to use it well requires that you practice humility, seek understanding and be thankful for your gift. Some people give false impressions to support their egos. With known talents there is less need to create false pretenses; therefore it is easier to be ethical, honest and considerate. You cannot help but be a better person, for knowing your talent will give you honest confidence. The joy of knowing your talent will make you a more contented person, someone who is likely to be more understanding of others.

Question: Will Talent Discovery make everyone talented?

Answer: Talent Discovery cannot make anyone something they are not; it will only open doors of opportunity for individuals, allowing them to realize their best abilities.

Question: Will everyone going through Talent Discovery come out knowing their talent?

Answer: Everyone can benefit learning more about themselves. Everyone has talent capability. Talent Discovery will identify as close as possible a person's maxtalability, to give them something worthwhile to work with.

Question: Will we want a world where everyone is talented and alike?

Answer: Everyone will not be alike. Society consists of a wide variety of people with different levels of desire to use their abilities. Some people may draw upon greater creative and motivational energies to apply their talents. Not all will use, learn or develop their talent in the same way. We will remain as individual and different as we are now.

Question: Will everyone's standard of living be equal?

Answer: Our average standard of living will be higher; and for most people as high as they want it to be. No two people with the same talent will be rewarded the same way. Some people are content with a simple life. Everyone has a different level of comfort, that will not change. In each occupation one person may lean towards writing, another teaching, researching, designing, illustrating or administrating. People have different personalities and levels of energy, ambition, motivation, and attention spans. The only equality will be in the opportunity to realize and utilize talent.

Question: Will everyone be wealthy?

Answer: Some people may choose to be wealthy and will work towards that end. Others may not. People are not in control of their income or work destiny now; they are at the mercy of the marketplace. People who know their talents will have more opportunity to control their working conditions and earnings. There should be fewer extremes and more equality in the compensation arena.

Question: How many people are now working in their maxtalability?

Answer: Unless our brain, genes and senses combined have an ability to discover maxtalability on their own, the discovery of maxtalability by instinct, grace or accident does not seem likely. With 40,000 occupations and the vast combinations of human activities it would be a rare happening.

Question: What about people who are now well-suited to their jobs, are successful and happy with their occupations?

Answer: Talent Discovery is not meant to disturb those who are happy and well-suited with their careers; although it could certainly compliment their career direction and open new doors to direct their careers, even in retirement. It can help them in their selection of hobbies and recreation. I have seen professional people who claim they love their jobs, when in actuality they were unchallenged and even bored. When they retired they did busy work, nothing they were deeply interested in. Knowing yourself better can be a valuable advantage throughout life.

Question: Do we have the technology to develop Talent Discovery?

Answer: Yes, we do. New technology is coming on-line so fast that some of the processes I described may already be subject to revision. Virtual reality is the answer to exposing an individual to work in areas that are too sensitive or dangerous for the unlicensed. Genetics is making substantial inroads, computer programming ability expands, and the exploration of the brain opens more doors. Robotics mimic and provide a source of human activity research and knowledge. Universities and colleges all over the world are working on areas that are basic and essential in the development of talent discovery. Fujitsu's Laboratories in Japan has as its slogan: 'What Mankind Can Dream, Technology Can Achieve.'

Question: What can we do while we wait for the talent booth to be developed?

Answer: See a career consultant. Learn about yourself. Take the available tests and research the occupations recommended. Use the 'Getting to know you' exercise to create like, indifferent and dislike lists of occupation job tasks and activities. You can make a start and begin to focus on some of your preferred job tasks. Some of you may even find that your talents could be used in developing Talent Discovery itself; and you could be in the forefront of this exciting new frontier.

26

Conclusion

*Today as a result of far reaching and technological
developments in our society, we are forced to
search for talent and to use it effectively. Among
the historic changes which have marked our era,
this may in the long run prove to be
one of the most profound.*

JOHN W. GARDNER, *EXCELLENCE*

The events leading to the development of Talent Discovery were described just as they happened. Breakthroughs took place in the most unlikely places and times, often missed completely or out of sequence. The most amazing observation about the Talent Discovery concept considering all the years it took to unravel, is that once computerized it is not very complicated at all.

Society has substantial problems. The problems are caused by faceless masses of people desperate for identity, personal value and a purpose in life. People create the problems, and only the talents of people can solve the problems. We are ruining our health, marriages, and families . . . killing ourselves trying to keep up by doing work we were not designed to do.

We shrug our shoulders and accept the fact that there is nothing we can do about it . . . that is the way it is. Is it?

Every year more than a 1,000,000 students drop out of school. Currently we will graduate 750,000 high school students who cannot read. Those 1,750,000 will join the 30,000,000 already classified as illiterate. There is a way to slow down and reverse this sad trend: find and educate students according to their talents and wrap the three R's around those talents. Discovered talents will not only reverse this trend but bring dropouts back to school.

The government has billions of dollars out in loans used to educate students in degrees in which they have little or no talent. Investing in Talent Discovery would be inexpensive insurance to back up these student loans.

Talent Discovery may be the common dedication needed to cross the lines of all nations. Global talent groupings will have a common purpose, the global glue that can override race, creed and color to provide the talent needed to solve global problems. It brings all humans of similar talent together in a brotherhood more important than any worldly conflict that individuals might otherwise become involved with.

There is no way we can lose investing in Talent Discovery, just turning the light on it and raising the question of hidden talents has value. Government and business should be in a rush to pull all stops to start Talent Discovery; it is less of a challenge than placing a man on the moon, and more beneficial to everyone. If we can penetrate the vastness of space we can penetrate a three pound brain, all we need is a reason. . . and now we have one.

There is no new invention to be developed, just a new combination of old procedures. If we can spend $25 billion for one man to walk on the moon, can't we spend far less for all individuals to have the right and dignity to walk on the path of their own talent?

What is it worth to improve the work value and quality of living of every individual? What is it worth to uncover millions of talents and experts to solve our trillion dollar problems? What is it worth to find hidden talents in potential terrorists; a talent that could provide them a better means of finding a positive identity and a better use of their energies and dedication? We cannot stop terrorists but talent discovery could provide an alternative to someone considering terrorism and criminal behavior.

New talents will result in new discoveries. High productivity from automation, robotics and energy from fusion or the sun should make living less expensive. People will work fewer hours and need less income to have an acceptable standard of living. Leisure time activities will become a greater part of our lives. Discovered talent will have to fill that time void if we are to be a healthy and free society.

Talent is ageless, it can renew and excite even the oldest people and provide them with new value, hope and respect. It is a mind craft science whose time has come. If we could jump ahead a hundred years I doubt that anyone would be in the jobs they are working at today because we will know so much more about natural ability.

There is little doubt that Talent Discovery will come into use and improve all of our lives. The day will come when men will not make a major move or a decision without checking the current status of their talent capabilities.

Like the Genome project to map our genes the Talent Discovery project needs interest, support and public demand to bring it into fruition. What is needed to start this project is a central committee of educators, government and business leaders to coordinate and develop the necessary procedures, equipment and financing. There is nothing a government can do that is more important than helping its citizens find their best talent and work value.

If we do not discover and learn to use the unique abilities each of us were given, humankind may be lost to an eternal purpose. The experiment of human life may be more important than we know. We must wake up, discover, and use our unique talents.

Talent discovery can free all people from intellectual and capability inequality and at the same time break the stubborn educational barrier to an efficient method of learning equitable for all people.

In this era of high technology man has realized that a person's genetic blueprint may be the key to more than his/her capabilities, that this unbiased blueprint may also be the key to their individuality, their purpose in life and what they were meant to accomplish.

We cannot know who we are or our purpose in life if we do not know our talents; the talents that will indicate what we can do best and what kind of a contribution we can make. All people deep down believe they are intelligent, special and capable, all they need is help to find what they can do best.

No matter what you the reader may conclude, concentrating scientific research on talent discovery can only produce important positive results that will help everyone in some way.

The twentieth century can usher in the renaissance of the individual through Talent Discovery . . . if we care enough and demand it be developed now.

Talent Discovery is the wonderful challenge that humankind is now faced with to uncover talents. The great reserves of undiscovered human talent are now discoverable. The beauty and wonder of self discovery awaits us all.

D.E.S.

Where there is no vision,
the people perish.

Proverbs 29:18

Bibliography

Ackerman, Diane. 1991. *A Natural History of the Senses* (New York: Vintage Books) p.xix.

Albus, James. 1981. *Brains Behavior, and Robotics* (Byte Publications Inc.) p.212.

Amabile, Teresa M. 1989. *Growing Up Creative* (New York: Crown Publishers Inc.) p.6.

Bolles, Richard Nelson. 1988. *What Color Is Your Parachute* (Berkeley: Ten Speed Press).

Bushnell, Horace, New England minister.

Clavell, James. 1993. *Gai Jin* (New York: Dell).

de Bono, Edward. 1992. *Serious Creativity* (New York: Harper Collins) p.310.

Fritz, Robert. 1989. *The Path of Least Resistance* (New York: Faucett Columbine) p.13.

Gallup Inc., *Reader's Digest*, May 1993, p.74.

Gardner, Howard. 1985. *Frames of Mind* (New York: Basic Books Inc.) pp.10, 34.

Gardner, John, W. 1962. *Excellence* (New York: Harper Rowe) pp.33, 105.

Gore, Al Senator. 1992. *Earth in Balance* (New York: Houghton Mifflin) p.367.

Gracian, Baltasar. Translated by Christopher Mauer.

Heim, Michael. 1993. *The Metaphysics of Virtual Reality* (New York: Oxford University Press) Foreword.

Kline, Peter. 1988. *The Everyday Genius* (Arlington: Great Ocean Publishers) pp.91, 184.

Kuder, Frederick. 1977. *Activity, Interests and Occupational Choice* (Lawrence Erlbaum Associates, Inc.) Section 6, pp.2, 182.

Montessori, Maria. May 22, 1937. Address given in Copenhagen.

Moore, Charles Guy. 1976. *The Career Game* (New York: National Institute of Career Planning) p.32.

Naisbitt, John and Patricia Aburdene. 1990. *Megatrends 2000* (New York: Avon Books) p.333.

Paepke, G. Owen. 1993. *The Evolution of Progress* (New York: Random House Press) p.xvii.

Rivilin, Robert and Karen Gravelle. 1984. *Deciphering the Senses* (New York: Simon & Schuster) p.25.

Scheinfeld, Amram. 1971. *Heredity in Humans.*

Shapiro, Robert. 1992. *The Human Blueprint* (New York: St. Martin's Press) p.278.

Shepard, Dr. Gordon. Yale University professor of neurobiology.

Sher, Barbara. 1994. *I Could Do Anything* (New York: Dell) p. 122

Stalnaker, John M. 1969. *The Discovery of Talent* (Cambridge: Harvard University Press) Bingham Lecture.

Sternberg, Robert and Janet E. Davidson. Edited by. 1986. *Conceptions of Giftedness* (New York: Cambridge University Press) p.125.

Strong, Edward K., Jr. 1943. *Vocational Interests of Men and Women* (Stanford: Stanford University Press) pp.17, 693.

Taylor, Gordon Rattray. 1979. *The Natural History of the Mind* (New York: Dutton) p.33.

U.S. Government, Department of Labor. 1977. *Dictionary of Occupations.*

U.S. Government, Department of Labor. 1988. *Occupational Outlook Handbook.*

Wheeler, John A., Physicist, *Reader's Digest*, September 1986, 107.

Wills, Christopher. 1989. *The Wisdom of the Genes* (New York: Basic Books) p.315.

Wolfe, Dael. Edited by. 1969. "The Discovery of Talent," *The Walter Van Dyke Bingham Lectures* (Cambridge: Harvard University Press) Part 3, Chapter 4.

Wolfe, Thomas Clayton. 1939. *The Web and the Rock,* Chapter 30.

Index